The **MindChamps Way**

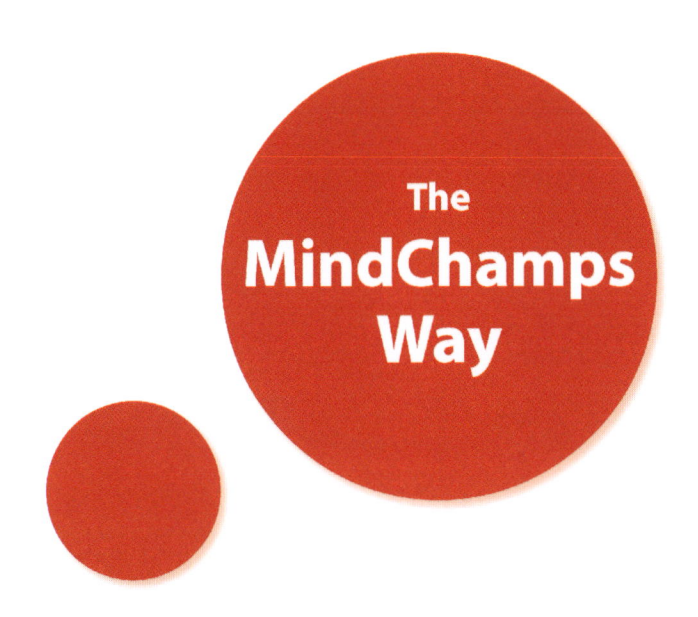

How to Turn An Idea Into A Global Movement

The MindChamps Way

How to Turn An Idea Into A Global Movement

Joseph A. Michelli

World Scientific

NEW JERSEY · LONDON · SINGAPORE · BEIJING · SHANGHAI · HONG KONG · TAIPEI · CHENNAI · TOKYO

Published by

World Scientific Publishing Co. Pte. Ltd.

5 Toh Tuck Link, Singapore 596224

USA office: 27 Warren Street, Suite 401-402, Hackensack, NJ 07601

UK office: 57 Shelton Street, Covent Garden, London WC2H 9HE

British Library Cataloguing-in-Publication Data
A catalogue record for this book is available from the British Library.

THE MINDCHAMPS WAY
How to Turn An Idea Into A Global Movement

Copyright © 2019 by World Scientific Publishing Co. Pte. Ltd.

All rights reserved. This book, or parts thereof, may not be reproduced in any form or by any means, electronic or mechanical, including photocopying, recording or any information storage and retrieval system now known or to be invented, without written permission from the publisher.

For photocopying of material in this volume, please pay a copying fee through the Copyright Clearance Center, Inc., 222 Rosewood Drive, Danvers, MA 01923, USA. In this case permission to photocopy is not required from the publisher.

ISBN 978-981-120-533-0

Desk Editor: Sandhya Venkatesh
Design and layout: Loo Chuan Ming

Printed in Singapore

*Author will donate all royalty proceeds
to The Jameson Foundation.*

CONTENTS

Special Message by The Hon Chris Bowen   vii

More Praises for the Book   xi

INTRODUCTION: **Education is the Future**   xiii

PART ONE – CREATING THE MOVEMENT

CHAPTER ONE
The "What" of MindChamps   3

CHAPTER TWO
"Right-Minded" Leadership & Expertise   17

CHAPTER THREE
From Purpose to Culture   37

PART TWO – DELIVERING THE MOVEMENT

CHAPTER FOUR
Champion, Learning, & Creative   67

CHAPTER FIVE
Driving Transformation and Growth   87

PART THREE – TAKING THE MOVEMENT TO THE WORLD

CHAPTER SIX
Producing Results   115

CHAPTER SEVEN
Shaping the Future   129

About the Author   143

Special Message by
The Hon Chris Bowen
Former Australian Treasurer, Current Shadow Treasurer

In the remarkable book you hold in your hands, Joseph Michelli, shares a quote from Nelson Mandela, the first President of the new South Africa. Mandela spoke from personal experience, when he pointed out that: "*Education is the most powerful weapon you can use to change the world.*"

The Information Revolution, which has exploded with such force over the past thirty years, means that we now exist in a rapidly-changing global environment. Faced with such volatility, therefore, it might be prudent to extend the great man's insight to read: "Education is also the most powerful weapon you can use to *keep pace with change in the world.*"

In the unpredictable future we have created for our children, individuals (and, indeed, nations) who merely maintain a standard, will find themselves falling behind at an accelerating rate. This means that rather than 'doubling down' on existing strategies – which most experts agree are not close to keeping pace with the current rate of change — education in tune with the 21st Century must look to the skills of creativity, critical-thinking, communication and collaboration and the 'mindset' of the enthusiastic, life-long learner.

Education systems world-wide spend billions annually in the search for better strategies, but change — for many legitimate reasons — tends to come slowly from within.

Throughout history, it seems that these types of breakthroughs actually require a different, more entrepreneurial, mindset to ignite the spark, and that mindset is the essential subject of *The MindChamps Way*.

It is a success-story, both in terms of the innovative educational model they have developed and the rapid success that has come with it, but this book looks behind the public success, to provide an insight into the personalities — and the mindsets — which underpin it.

Some years ago, an old friend made me aware of MindChamps, and I was impressed with their approach of identifying 'gaps' in society — especially in education — and working creatively to find ways of filling them. After reading *The 3-Mind Revolution* by David Chiem and Brian Caswell, I commented that it was 'a thought-provoking and easy-to-read guide to what is necessary to prosper in an information-rich world.'

A decade on, and the 'revolution' which they advocated has become an expanding global movement.

The MindChamps Way traces that growth, the foundational strategies, the leadership and the underlying philosophy driving it, but it also allows us insight into the values and the social charter which define the organization.

SPECIAL MESSAGE BY THE HON CHRIS BOWEN

In order to be an agent for change from a position beyond government, first and foremost, you must be successful, and in an environment as competitive and demanding as international education, this requires a strong business model, scalable protocols and world-class branding — but education is not like any other 'business'.

The MindChamps Way demonstrates that by deliberately placing the values of Heart and Integrity above Prosperity, Growth and Expansion, this 'revolutionary' organization has set in motion the change that they imagined possible twenty years ago — to (in the words of their Vision and Social Charter), 'challenge and improve education standards globally' and '[create] educational opportunities where they would not otherwise exist.'

The MindChamps Way is a success-story with heart, that traces the links between future-paced strategy, commercial success and social responsibility — which is a model we can all aspire to.

Canberra, 2019.

More Praises for the Book

"David Chiem is one of the most insightful and forward-thinking people I have come to know, and respect, in my life.

His approach to educating our next generation of leaders recognises the challenges and opportunities of our changing world and teaches adaptability and agility so as to make the most of future times, no matter what lies ahead.

He is deeply passionate about the objectives of MindChamps and how a commitment to the 'right' early learning can make the world a better place."

Dr Roger Sexton
Executive Chairman, Beston Pacific Asset

"MindChamps' passion to make a meaningful and positive change in society is indeed worthy of emulation. As this book demonstrates, MindChamps is helping to lay the foundation for successful, long-term outcomes in learning. SGX is excited to be MindChamp's fund-raising partner, as it pursues its global vision to enable equitable opportunities and access to quality education for children in Singapore and around the world."

Mr Loh Boon Chye
CEO, Singapore Exchange

I read The MindChamps Way with great interest. It contains great insight into education, focussing on preparing the whole person, from an early age.

Education consists of more than the mere accumulation of knowledge. Never has this been more true than at a time when everybody, thanks to SmartPhones and the search engines – and now, Artificial Intelligence – has at their fingertips any facts they may dream of. The MindChamps Way is a great study of the philosophy and strategies of what it takes to build a successful global education movement.

Mr Wolfgang Bertelsmeier
Chairman Veil Capital

I read The MindChamps Way in one day. The reason I found it so compelling is that David Chiem and his colleagues have set the foundations in MindChamps 1.0 and 2.0 as effective learning platforms for a new era that is about to arrive – which will no doubt be reflected in MindChamps 3.0. My field is developing software robots that amplify systems and augment humans. We build brains made from algorithms and neural networks that humans will partner with in school, at home and at work. These software robots will fundamentally change the way children and adults learn, how they work and the jobs they do. Is the current schooling system and curriculum preparing young people for the future? Absolutely not. It is time to revolutionise learning and this book both lays the foundations and creates the movement to do so. I applaud the MIndChamps team and commend Michelli on creating this book in order to further this amazing work. Congratulations!

Dr Catriona Wallace
CEO & Founder Flamingo AI
Artificial Intelligence & Bot Strategist
Australian Financial Review's Most Influential Woman in Business & Entrepreneurship

INTRODUCTION
Education is the Future

Our greatest natural resource is in the minds of our children.

Walt Disney
Co-founder of The Walt Disney Company

What's In this For You?

Swiss psychologist Jean Piaget observed, "The goal of education is not to increase the amount of knowledge but to create the possibilities for a child to invent and discover, to create men who are capable of doing new things."

This is a book about MindChamps, a business in the education sector which shares Piaget's view on the importance of helping children create possibilities for invention and discovery. However, for the people who founded and helped MindChamps grow, and for the countless lives touched by the brand, MindChamps is more than a business—it is a calling, a revolution, and a movement. It started from a simple yet bold desire to change the world for the better – to fill in one of the most important gaps on the planet; "a gap that has the most direct impact on the future of our world and our species."

The MindChamps Way is written for diverse but related audiences including business readers, investors, parents, teachers, educators, and those concerned about both the future of education and equitable access to quality educational opportunities. As a business author and consultant, I've spent most of my career working with and writing about industry-leading companies such as Starbucks, Mercedes-Benz, and The Ritz-Carlton Hotel Company.

The MindChamps Way, like eight of my prior books, is written to help business leaders, managers, and frontline employees gain insights from this extraordinary company. As such, this book offers business lessons which have been culled from MindChamps' leadership. These insights are based on concepts, actions, and tools used by MindChamps' leaders to steward their company from ambition to global success in a relatively short period of time.

Having conducted research for my master's degree and Ph.D. in Clinical Psychology through the Family Studies Program at the University of Southern California, I have also published research articles and practical tools related to psychology, family communication, and parenting skills, including a book titled, "***Humor, Play & Laughter: Stress-Proofing Life with Your Kids***." Given my own interest in children and education, I've written ***The MindChamps Way*** to offer insights from MindChamps' leaders on how to solve important issues in education. Moreover, ***The MindChamps Way*** offers a perspective on the transformative impact MindChamps is having on parents, teachers, and the educational system globally.

The Structure

This book is written in three sections across seven chapters. Part

INTRODUCTION

one, titled "**Creating the Movement**," focuses on the origins, people, and culture of MindChamps. This section is comprised of three chapters. The first chapter, "**The 'What' of MindChamps**," addresses the company's evolution and growth. Chapter two, "**Right-Minded Leadership & Expertise**," introduces you to the company's founder, CEO and Executive Chairman Mr. David Chiem, and examines how his leadership qualities positioned the company for success. This chapter also looks at the breadth and depth of experts who are helping MindChamps build educational tools to meet 21st Century needs. Chapter three, "**From Purpose to Culture**," looks at MindChamps' mission, vision, and values and how those cultural elements are nurtured and activated throughout the organization.

Part two, titled "**Delivering the Movement**," focuses on MindChamps' research, learning model, curriculum, and educational effectiveness. The content of this section is delivered across two chapters. Chapter four, "**Champion, Learning and Creative**," shows how the information age and technological advances produce an urgent need for dramatic educational improvements guided by breakthrough scientific research. It will also help you understand how MindChamps has built a learning model that positions children for success in a rapidly changing world. In Chapter five, "**Driving Transformation and Growth**," you will learn how MindChamps translates its evidence-based learning constructs into engaging and effective curriculum. Moreover, you will see how that curriculum is managed with turnkey consistency and efficiency.

The last two chapters of the book make up part three, titled "**Taking the Movement to the World**." This section looks at MindChamps' global impact and explores the likely legacy of the brand. In Chapter six, "**Producing Results**," I'll share a combination of outcome data and personal stories about MindChamps' educational and social influence. To assess MindChamps' efficacy, you will read the words of students, parents, educators, investors, and community leaders. Chapter seven, "**Shaping the Future**," examines MindChamps' goals and opportunities and will offer you a chance to synthesize information provided throughout the book. Before we learn about and from MindChamps, let's take a moment to appreciate the societal significance of early childhood education.

Where it Matters Most

I have been fortunate to consult for many highly recognizable global brands. Of the many companies with whom I've worked, I choose to write books about those that are having a transformative effect on their respective industries. In addition to working with Starbucks, Mercedes-Benz, and The Ritz-Carlton Hotel Company, as noted above, I have also written about the world-famous Pike Place Fish Market in Seattle, UCLA Health Systems, Zappos, and Airbnb. The aforementioned global brands have effectively disrupted or established trends in travel, retail, automotive, healthcare, and hospitality sectors. Some of them, like Starbucks and Airbnb, have seen their brand name become synonymous with the products they sell. For example, it's not unusual to hear someone say, "Let's grab a Starbucks," when they mean "Let's get a coffee." Similarly, a traveler might say, "I'm going to look for an Airbnb," when they are considering a short-term rental.

While the companies featured in my prior books demonstrate impressive brand power, none of them have been in a position to fundamentally shape society on par with MindChamps. Given

INTRODUCTION

its industry, MindChamps is influencing the future of individuals, families, communities, countries, and the education system worldwide. The former President of South Africa, anti-apartheid crusader, and revolutionary Nelson Mandela put it this way: "Education is the most powerful weapon which you can use to change the world."

Given education's potential to positively drive social change, parents and leaders must invest wisely in educational resources that maximize return. According to 2U, a company that provides digital educational resources to colleges and universities, more than 1.9 trillion dollars is spent every year on higher education globally. While post-secondary education helps prepare young adults for an increasingly complex world, investments in early childhood education have been shown to produce greater economic and social returns.

As you'll learn in chapter one, MindChamps' research from the late 1990s identified a gap in education which required solutions for children in their most formative years. These early insights were later validated by the University of Chicago's Nobel Prize winning economist, Professor James Heckman. Professor Heckman found the essential time to offer quality educational opportunities is between birth and age five. Based on his research, Professor Heckmen concludes that this is "when the brain develops rapidly to build the foundation of cognitive and character skills necessary for success in school, health, career and life. Early childhood education fosters cognitive skills along with attentiveness, motivation, self-control and sociability—the character skills that turn knowledge into know-how and people into productive citizens."

To understand the importance of factors that affect long-term

xix

educational outcomes, University of Oxford economist and founder of "Our World in Data" Max Roser and Esteban Ortiz-Ospina (who is also an economist at the University of Oxford) produced a lengthy report titled "Global Rise of Education." Their analysis was designed to provide "an overview of long run changes in education outcomes and outputs across the world, focusing both on quantity and quality measures of education attainment; and then provide an analysis of available evidence on the determinants and consequences of education." In their final conclusions for "Our World in Data," these analysts note, "A number of studies have found that it is actually education in the form of cognitive skills, rather than mere school attainment, that really matters for predicting individual earnings and economic growth."

In addition to cognitive skills, Professor Heckman's work emphasizes social skill development early in the educational process. He recommends parents and community leaders, "Invest in the 'whole child.' Effective early childhood education packages cognitive skills with character skills such as attentiveness, impulse control, persistence and teamwork. Together, cognition and character drive education, career and life success—with character development often being the most important factor."

To summarize the above-referenced research (e.g., that of MindChamps, Professor Heckman, and economists Roser/Ortiz-Ospina) investments in education optimally should be targeted to young learners. Those investments should focus less on knowledge acquisition and more on cognitive and social skill development. The returns from investments in quality skills-based early education have been shown to be sizable. They are demonstrated at the individual level through long-term education, career, and life success and

INTRODUCTION

also have impact at a societal level by driving literacy and global economic growth.

In chapters four and five, we will explore MindChamps' revolutionary approach for helping children develop thinking and social skills. However, let's take a moment to look at an earlier revolution in early childhood education. Relatively speaking, teaching young children is a fairly young industry. Most people credit Freidrich Froebel, the creator of the first kindergarten in Germany in 1837, as spearheading early childhood learning.

According to the Director of Graduate Business Programs at Alverno College Professor Stephani Richards-Wilson, Froebel experimented for nearly fifty years to develop and implement his educational system, which put him squarely at odds with conventional educational theory. Professor Richards-Wilson notes Froebel's "new child-centered approach differed from extant educational practices and societal views in which young children were often disciplined as defective or miniature adults. Froebel was convinced that they were inherently good-natured, should be granted the freedom to self-govern, and had the intelligence and aptitude to learn through creative, imaginative, and spontaneous play. He believed that children could teach themselves lessons about harmony and beauty by playing with form, shapes, and color." Froebel explored child development for children from ages three to six—an age group previously believed to be incapable of conventional school work.

Almost two centuries later, MindChamps continues in the educational tradition of Froebel. Like their German predecessor, the leaders at MindChamps spent a considerable amount of time developing and implementing their research-based educational system. Similarly, MindChamps' leadership has challenged conventional educational theory as they seek to revolutionize solutions on behalf of current and future generations.

I titled this introduction "**Education is the Future**" to highlight an emerging consensus reflected by researchers, economists, and global leaders. That consensus is expressed in the thinking of professor, author, advocate, and futurist, Dr. Matthew Lynch. Writing in *The Edvocate*, Professor Lynch notes, "Early childhood education is the foundation of our society. If we do not set children up to succeed, they will ultimately fail. The failure of future generations would be the downfall of our social and economic structure. This is a concept which is now widely accepted. And, many countries have implemented programs to encourage and support early learners."

The benefits of quality early childhood education and ongoing quality learning experiences are summarized by the U.S. Centers for Disease Control (CDC). The CDC, consistent with Dr. Heckman's research, reports that children who are provided quality learning opportunities early in life demonstrate improved cognitive development, emotional development, self-regulation, and academic achievement. The CDC also indicates other social benefits, which include:

"Savings from reduced grade retention
Savings in health care costs
Savings in remedial education and child care costs
Improvement in health outcomes associated with education
Earnings gains associated with high school graduation
Better jobs and higher earnings throughout employment years for children participating in these programs

INTRODUCTION

…other positive health effects, including healthier weight (such as fewer underweight, overweight, and obese children)."

Given the critical importance of delivering quality early learning experiences, you will soon see how MindChamps is consistently offering premium early childhood education on a global scale. You will also appreciate how MindChamps has redesigned learning for the modern age.

Why was a new approach needed? In an article for *Edsurge Independent*, teacher Abigail Cox observed, "The current educational system was designed during the agrarian era and only slightly modified during industrial times…it was created with the intent of imparting values and skills of these times onto students. The transition between the agrarian and industrial eras was influenced by the ideology that public education was the best method of teaching unruly children discipline. Today, our school system still values discipline and a structured regimen under the teacher's discretion. Today our schools are still teaching many of the same values, but with yesterday's methods." In chapter four, MindChamps leaders will share their perspective on how information proliferation and technological advancement necessitate an educational revolution devoid of agrarian and industrial age approaches.

At this point you may be feeling that it is hard enough to run a business or help your own children and grandchildren realize the fullness of their potential, let alone improve the global educational system. Thanks to the insights you will gain from MindChamps, I hope this book helps you learn, create, and champion your business, your family, and our world. To embark on that journey,

I am reminded of advice shared by writer and humorist Samuel Clemens, when he observed "the secret of getting ahead is getting started. The secret of getting started is breaking your complex overwhelming tasks into small manageable tasks, then starting on the first one." Let's take a small manageable step by examining the origins of MindChamps, the company's meteoric growth, and the brand's accomplishments and recognitions.

The future awaits. It's time to dive in and orient ourselves to MindChamps!

PART ONE

CREATING
THE MOVEMENT

CHAPTER ONE

The "What" of MindChamps

Go into the world and do well. But more importantly, go into the world and do good.

Minor Myers
Yale University Law Professor

When I wrote my book, **The New Gold Standard: 5 Leadership Principles for Creating a Legendary Customer Experience Courtesy of The Ritz-Carlton Hotel Company**, I traced the history of The Ritz-Carlton Hotel chain back to 1870. Much of that brand's commitment to elevated service excellence is reflected in the thinking and words of the company's founder Cesar Ritz, who noted extraordinary means "to see all without looking; to hear all without listening; to be attentive without being servile; to anticipate without being presumptuous."

Like the Ritz-Carlton, MindChamps' commitment to excellence (in areas of research, education design, and scalable learning environments) links to its founder David Chiem. During a conversation with David, he shared "From the onset, I've wanted to change the world for the better and use my passion for education combined with experiences in the creative arts to fundamentally improve the way children learn. MindChamps emerged from a desire to enable consistent quality education for every child." While both Cesar Ritz and David Chiem have built businesses that strive for transformational excellence, there is one fundamental difference between MindChamps and The Ritz Carlton Hotel Company. That difference relates to the speed by which MindChamps has catapulted to international prominence.

From Australia to Singapore

In 1998, MindChamps began as an educational research center in Sydney, Australia. At that time, MindChamps' founder David Chiem and a small group of colleagues began exploring questions about gaps in education. David notes, "We studied educational delivery and saw lots of local and regional approaches attempting to maximize the potential of students. We benchmarked the best approaches, immersed ourselves in outcome data, and tried to understand the shortcomings in efforts to address what clearly was a global need. Four areas stood out to us. The mindset of the learner was often overlooked, a great deal of emphasis was being placed on the content of learning, the delivery system was outdated, and a single discipline solution typically was being attempted when a multi-disciplinary approach was needed." In response to their observations, David and his team began soliciting the input of experts from a multiplicity of disciplines including education, psychology, neuroscience, and theater (some of whom are spotlighted in chapter two). This input was used to develop a model of learning and possible strategies for building skills relevant to emerging societal needs.

MindChamps started testing their learning tools with primary school age children, but David notes, "We began to see that by

CHAPTER ONE

primary school, many children had already formed habits and beliefs about their ability to learn. This made it more difficult for them to progress as rapidly as they could have if someone had offered them tools to develop more effective skills and a more constructive learning mindset." For several years, MindChamps continued to prototype learning concepts in Australia through freestanding programs.

In 2002, MindChamps began testing its learning solutions in Singapore and established its corporate office there. When asked why MindChamps moved its headquarters to Singapore, David shared, "Since we were seeking to address educational needs globally, we decided to take our approach to a country that reflects a special blend of Eastern and Western cultures; a country that is the gateway to the world. We also knew Singapore had a high achieving education system that also reflected traditional learning approaches and their system emphasized educational content as opposed to learning process. We believed that if our new model could achieve success in Singapore, it would be a springboard for revolutionizing education globally." MindChamps produced outstanding outcomes from freestanding learning initiatives (with titles like "Success 4 Life") in Singapore, which paved the way in 2008 for the next phase in MindChamps' evolution.

The Birth of the MindChamps PreSchool and Franchise

The first decade in MindChamps history (1998 – 2008) could be described as researching problems and solutions, developing testable and multi-disciplinary educational innovation, and prototyping an effective delivery system across both Australia and Singapore. As David puts it, "When we first began our journey, I believed it would take about a decade to research, build, test, and perfect a solution before we could make it available in a way that could credibly allow us to share our story and tools on a broad scale." That broad scale sharing occurred in 2008 with the launch of MindChamps' first PreSchool in Singapore and the beginning of MindChamps' franchise model.

Based on the strength of MindChamps' reputation for educational excellence, before opening the first MindChamps PreSchool, it had reached capacity and had 150 students on its waiting list. David says, "From the beginning, we wanted to create early learning solutions that could scale globally. Plus, I knew PreSchools must be local. Parents might travel to take their children to excellent high schools and people travel away for outstanding opportunities when it comes to college, but parents need a premium PreSchool near where they work and live. Given our global goal and the local needs of families, I knew we needed to have a scalable solution. As we designed our first PreSchool, we built it so it could be distributed into local communities throughout the world through a franchise model. We would keep tight quality controls on the model, but we wanted to partner with others to take the model throughout Singapore and the world."

MindChamps began sharing the opportunity to bring its learning solutions to like-minded leaders and entrepreneurs even before their first PreSchool officially opened. To the amazement of many franchise experts, at the same time MindChamps opened its first PreSchool, the company had signed franchise agreements for 22 PreSchools in Singapore. These franchise agreements proved to be in high demand due to the reputation MindChamps had

CHAPTER ONE

earned through its dedication to research and the success of its freestanding enrichment offerings.

The success of the launch was featured on the front cover of Asia Franchise, because of the way that it broke with convention, by selling 22 licences before opening its first school. This is a common theme in the MindChamps story — breaking with conventional ways of operating, to take 'the path less chosen'.

Today, MindChamps operates four separate segments for the Early-Childhood Division:

- **PreSchool** – This is MindChamps' flagship division, offering award-winning PreSchool education and enrichment programs to children ages eighteen months to six years and world-class Infant Care for children from six to eighteen months.

- **Chinese PreSchool** – Based on MindChamps' original PreSchool program, MindChamps Chinese PreSchool serves parents who want their children to acquire a solid foundation in the Chinese language.

- **Reading and Writing** – The MindChamps Reading and Writing program offers highly-engaging enrichment focused on literacy. The reading program is available for children ages three to six, and the writing program serves children ages six to ten.

- **MindChamps Music** – Developed using over 3 decades of research and the unique expertise of Dr. Larry Scripp – one of the world's leading authorities on Music in Education, MindChamps Music is a totally new, integrative approach to developing musical literacy and supporting numeracy and language acquisition in very young children.

By 2009, within a year of commencing operations, MindChamps PreSchool had won the Promising Franchisor of the Year Award from the Franchising and Licensing Association of Singapore. Two years later, in 2011, MindChamps expanded its PreSchool offering and franchise opportunities by launching the MindChamps Reading and Writing program. That curriculum, a set of freestanding enrichment offerings, blended into the MindChamps PreSchool curriculum by 2012.

Along the way, MindChamps achieved industry and brand awards (which I will spotlight later in this chapter), but more importantly, the company managed growth and expanded the impact of its learning tools to increasing numbers of Singaporean families. By October 2013, MindChamps had twenty PreSchools operating in Singapore (eighteen of which were franchise operations). By August 2014, MindChamps had opened thirty-one PreSchools and reading and writing centers across Singapore.

In 2014, MindChamps' leadership announced that they would partner with media powerhouse Singapore Press Holdings (SPH) to expand the MindChamps education model globally. The CEO of SPH, Alan Chan, stated that SPH had spent eight years seeking an education partner that could 'go global' and that after looking into every sector of education, none had stood up to what they found in MindChamps PreSchool. "MindChamps PreSchool," he wrote, "is well-positioned with its proprietary teaching methodology and management system to meet the demand for pre-school and enrichment programmes in Singapore and abroad."

We will discuss both MindChamps' proprietary teaching methodology and management system in later chapters; however, it should be acknowledged that Mr. Chan was absolutely correct

CHAPTER ONE

in his assessment of how well MindChamps was positioned for foreign growth.

As of 2018, MindChamps' reach expanded from Singapore to Australia, the Philippines, Abu Dhabi, Dubai, Myanmar, Vietnam, and Malaysia. Also in 2018, MindChamps launched a major Education Symposium at the Bird's Nest (National Olympic Stadium) stadium in Beijing, to position its education model into China.

When I asked David about MindChamps' global footprint, he noted, "It's never been about footprint for us. I think brands that focus only on footprint often shoot themselves in the foot. We've always set out to produce educational results and a process that delivers the best educational solution possible. We've found that when we do that, leaders across the world come to us asking to provide the MindChamps innovation in their communities. We have experienced growth based on a sound reputation not by seeking a targeted footprint. We have built a global solution and the world is hearing our story. The response has been strong and steady." MindChamps' "strong and steady" growth will invariably extend beyond Australia and Asia, as the company is poised to respond to interest throughout Europe and the Western Hemisphere.

Rather than taking you through all the brand's milestones, I will jump ahead to some of the most significant events in MindChamps' recent history. As of July 11, 2018, MindChamps PreSchool had sold 165 licenses under both unit and master franchise agreements. By the end of 2018, MindChamps had opened 74 centers. In 2018 alone, the company opened seven new centers in Australia, three in Singapore, and a new center in Dubai, the Philippines, Myanmar, and Vietnam. While there is so much that can be written about MindChamps' short but significant history, let's examine MindChamps' journey to becoming a publicly traded company and the overall reach of its business.

In addition to engaging entrepreneurs through franchise agreements, MindChamps' leaders enabled investors an opportunity to participate in the company's growth, expansion, and earning potential. On November 10, 2017, MindChamps' leaders lodged their preliminary prospectus with the Monetary Authority of Singapore, proposing an initial public offering (IPO) to list ordinary shares in MindChamps PreSchool Limited on the Mainboard of the Singapore Exchange Securities Trading Limited.

In their November 17, 2017, announcement of their IPO, MindChamps reported subscription by three high-quality investors, CFCG Investment Partners International (Singapore) Pte. Ltd., the Hillhouse Funds, and Target Asset Management Pte Ltd., for an aggregate of 28,930,800 Cornerstone Shares. As for the formal offering (subject to an overallotment option), MindChamps noted that it was seeking S$49.3 million in capital investment by offering 30,449,600 shares at S$0.83.

MindChamps offered an aggregate of 28,449,600 shares to institutional and other investors in Singapore (of which 2,438,000 shares were reserved for management, employees, and other business associates who contributed to MindChamps' success) and 2,000,000 shares to the public.

On November 23, 2017, MindChamps reported an overwhelming response to its IPO:

"At the close of the Public Offering at 12 noon (Singapore time) on 22 November 2017, 5,282 valid applications for a total of 165,949,000 Public Offer Shares amounting to

CHAPTER ONE

approximately S$137.7 million were received, resulting in the Public Offer being approximately 83.0 times subscribed.

This made MindChamps PreSchool the first, and only, preschool organization to be successfully listed on the main board of the stringent Singapore stock exchange.

MindChamps' IPO demonstrated that the company was extremely attractive to both institutional and public investors, prompting the Executive Chairman of MindChamps PreSchool Limited and the MindChamps Founder and CEO David Chiem to reflect that, "The positive demand from both institutional and retail investors is a strong testament to MindChamps Preschools' unique investment proposition and cutting-edge 3-Mind education model... The successful listing is an important milestone in our efforts to empower more students with the values, mindset and skills to achieve their full potential in life. Going forward, we will continue to uphold and maintain our reputation for excellence and deliver long-term value to all our stakeholders—from students, to parents and shareholders alike."

David's commitment to empower more students is reflected in the company's scope. That scope is best measured in the number of lives touched by MindChamps. In Singapore alone, MindChamps is number one in market share among the country's premium PreSchools. It presently commands 38.5% of that market.

MindChamps' rapid growth has widened the brand's overall impact. Since its inception, more than 100,000 students have graduated from MindChamps programs. Currently, the MindChamps brand has provided over 10,000 jobs to those working for the company and its franchisees. If you consider all the family members of MindChamps graduates and related employees, you begin to appreciate the company's impact! MindChamps' impact can also be inferred through the independent awards and honors received by the company and its leaders.

Awards and Honors–MindChamps Recognized as a Champion

French mathematician, inventor, and writer Blaise Pascal is credited with communicating an idea that has been popularized to read: "If I had more time, I would have written a shorter letter." For me, that phrase reflects the importance of taking the time to condense written information.

When I first sought to capture MindChamps' accomplishments in this section, it resulted in a very wordy draft. However, guided by Pascal's wisdom, I significantly shortened the MindChamps award section. Please understand that in doing so, you are only being exposed to a portion of MindChamps' awards and honors. I have arranged the following in reverse chronological order and omitted entries where MindChamps had prior wins in a particular category.

2018
- **Top Brand** – Conferred by Influential Brands®.
- **Top Employer Brand** – Received from Influential Brands®.
- **Hall of Fame Inductee** – A result of winning Influential Brands® Top Brand award for five consecutive years.
- **Asia's Greatest Leaders Award (David Chiem)** – presented by AsiaOne Magazine & PriceWaterhouseCoopers.
- **Asia's Greatest Brands Award (MindChamps)** – presented by AsiaOne Magazine & PriceWaterhouseCoopers.

- **Superbrands Mark of Distinction (Early Learning and Preschool category)** – This represented MindChamps' fifth consecutive award from Superbrands.

2017
- **Ranked #8 on the 2017 Enterprise 50 Award** – This is based on MindChamps' ability to innovate, lead, and manage when benchmarked against peers and other contemporaries.
- **Dun & Bradstreet Business Eminence Award** – MindChamps is among "the best and highest achievers in their industry."

2016
- The inaugural **2016 CEO Brand Leader of the Year Award** to Mr. David Chiem—This is awarded to a handful of business leaders who demonstrate "strong business leadership and have fully embraced branding as part of their business strategy." The award is presented to recipients who deliver brand leadership, brand expansion, financial performance, innovation, and personal integrity.
- **Intellectual Property Office of Singapore's (IPOS) Trademark Portfolio of the Year award** – Conferred by the regulatory body in charge of intellectual property for Singapore.
- **Placed amongst the top 1% of Singapore's leading corporations and SMEs** – This represents the fifth consecutive year MindChamps placed in this percentile based on "stringent and intensive reviews of over 70,000 audited financials obtained from the Accounting and Corporate Regulatory Authority of Singapore (ACRA)."

2015 and prior
- **Outstanding Entrepreneur Award at the Asia Pacific Entrepreneurship Awards** – Given to Mr. David Chiem from a large field of leaders from all industries, for business achievements over three financial years.
- **Top Entrepreneur of the Year Award** – Bestowed by Rotary Club Association of Small and Medium Enterprises (ASME).
- **Franchisor of the Year 2013** – Awarded by the Franchising & Licensing Association. This award includes all global franchise brands.
- **Rising Star Brand Award** – Conferred by Brand Finance.

The slate of awards outlined above is a strong validation of MindChamps' quality leadership and brand success.

As much as awards are appreciated by individuals and business leaders, those who oversee MindChamps prefer to focus on the company's mission and purpose. This is reflected in comments like those made by the company's CEO David Chiem upon winning the Dun and Bradstreet award, "While our business numbers and financial growth have garnered recognition from Dun and Bradstreet and earned us this award, for us at MindChamps, we have always believed that the numbers mean nothing unless we are truly making a difference to society through education."

David's comments reflect keen insight in keeping with observations made by businessman and author Robert Kiyosaki, who noted, "Most businesses think that product is the most important thing, but without great leadership, mission and a team that delivers results at a high level, even the best product won't make a company successful." In the next two chapters, we will

CHAPTER ONE

further explore MindChamps' leadership, pursuit of knowledge, and dedication to mission.

Before we advance to the next chapter, let's summarize some possible takeaways, and look for applications of content from this chapter as well as from the introduction. At the end of this and each ensuing chapter, you will find a "Follow the Red Dot" section. The Red Dot refers to MindChamps' Brand Symbol. I trust that by following the Red Dot you will benefit from **The MindChamps Way**.

Follow the Red Dot

- Education involves more than the acquisition of knowledge. It is a process that enables thinking skills as well as the ability to invent and discover. How can you apply this insight to your organization?
- How might you follow in the tradition of Freidrich Froebel and the thought leaders behind MindChamps, to challenge convention, experiment with ideas, and prototype new product offerings?
- Where do you have opportunities to upgrade the outdated and revolutionize solutions for the modern age?
- In what areas of your life are you taking the time to study, benchmark, ideate, test, and scale?
- When it comes to business success, how are you driving organic growth built on reputation?
- From a business perspective, how effectively are you expanding your product offerings and brand reach?
- In what ways is your success linked to the opportunities you create for others.
- Strive for excellence and enjoy the rewards that follow. As virologist and inventor of the polio vaccine, Jonas Salk, said, realize "the reward for work well done is the opportunity to do more."
- Touch lives and above all else, in the words of David Chiem, "truly make a difference."

CHAPTER TWO

"Right-Minded" Leadership & Expertise

Start small, think big. Don't worry about too many things at once. Take a handful of simple things to begin with, and then progress to more complex ones. Think about not just tomorrow, but the future. Put a ding in the universe.

Steve Jobs
Chief Executive Officer and Co-founder of Apple Inc.

Chapter one told the high-level story of MindChamps, an expansion story staged in the span of two decades. It reflects the journey of an idea in the mind of MindChamps' founder into a multinational, rapidly growing, publicly-traded, well-capitalized, market leader. Many of the decisions that led to MindChamps' success can be traced directly to leadership qualities forged in the character and mindset of its founder, David Chiem.

In this chapter, we will explore the concept of mindset and the benefits companies achieve when their leaders develop mindsets that foster achievement, learning, and creativity. We will examine David Chiem's life journey to see how his successful mindset emerged. We will close the chapter by learning about some of the talented global authorities and advisors who guide MindChamps' evolution. David Chiem has said, "It all begins with mindset." Spurred by David's wisdom, let's begin by exploring the science behind that construct.

The Science of Mindset

While many theorists and researchers have explored the concept of mindset, there has been an upsurge in the topic's popularity, thanks in large measure to the research and writings of Stanford professor and psychologist Carol Dweck. Professor Dweck's book, *Mindset: The New Psychology of Success*, is a must-read for anyone seeking to learn more about productive and counter-productive perspectives. Bill Gates, principle founder of the Microsoft Corporation, described Professor Dweck's book by noting, "Through clever research studies and engaging writing, Dweck illuminates how our beliefs about our capabilities exert tremendous influence on how we learn and which paths we take in life." As you'll learn later, Professor Dweck's research and expertise validates views which have been long-held by David Chiem and other MindChamps' leaders.

Throughout her body of work, Professor Dweck likens mindsets to self-perceptions or internal dialogues. For example, people form perspectives about their abilities in areas like drawing or public speaking. According to Professor Dweck, individuals who believe these types of characteristics are resistant to change, exert less effort to grow or develop them. In other words, if a person sees themselves as lacking artistic talent, and if they believe that talent is innate, that person typically won't enroll in a drawing class. According to Professor Dweck, such a person would be said to have a fixed mindset. Conversely, people who are constantly seeking to learn, grow, and improve are said to have a growth mindset.

In *Mindset: The New Psychology of Success*, Professor Dweck notes, "The passion for stretching yourself and sticking to it, even (or especially) when it's not going well, is the hallmark of

CHAPTER TWO

the growth mindset. This is the mindset that allows people to thrive during some of the most challenging times in their lives." (As you will learn later in the chapter, this ability to learn from adversity is also foundational both to David Chiem's development and to a MindChamps concept referred to as the "Champion Mindset.") According to Professor Dweck's research, this tendency to adopt a growth vs. fixed mindset changes the course of one's life and even one's happiness.

In an article for ***Scientific American*** titled "The Secret to Raising Smart Kids," Professor Dweck concludes that growth-oriented mindsets produce champions in "almost every human endeavor. For instance, many young athletes value talent more than hard work and have consequently become unteachable. Similarly, many people accomplish little in their jobs without constant praise and encouragement to maintain their motivation. If we foster a growth mind-set in our homes and schools, however, we will give our children the tools to succeed in their pursuits and to become productive workers and citizens." Dr. Dweck's research on the importance of fostering healthy, adaptive mindsets in children (so they have the tools to succeed in their pursuits) is at the core of why MindChamps exists. It also represents a core quality of David Chiem and one of MindChamps' most significant contributions to global education.

In their book, ***The 3-Mind Revolution—A New World View for Global Leaders, Educators and Parents***, David Chiem and MindChamps' Dean of Research and Programme Development Brian Caswell write about their work with Professor Allan Snyder (much more on him later in this chapter) to isolate components of mindset that lead to success, then find ways to translate that knowledge into practical and effective teaching and learning strategies.

David shares: "At MindChamps, we have always believed that everything we do, if it is to be effective long-term, must go both deep and wide. Working with Allan Snyder, we assembled the research from his extensive work with world leading achievers like Nelson Mandela, Sir Richard Branson and Oliver Sacks; the experiences and strategies of high-achievers in all fields, from sports to business, the arts to politics and science, and the important insights drawn from the ground-breaking Olympic Cultural Event forums, 'What Makes a Champion?' at both the Sydney 2000 and the Beijing 2008 Olympics and the 'What Makes a Young Champion?' event at the inaugural Youth Olympics in Singapore, 2010. We looked for ways to 'weaponize' what we had discovered in the search for a better way to prepare young people for success in an unknowable future, and built the results of our search into every aspect of the MindChamps 3 Minds approach."

This work is succinctly captured in the MindChamps construct of the Champion Mindset:

"Champion Mindset is another area of groundbreaking research, undertaken over the last 20 years, by Professor Snyder. Its basic elements are outlined in his seminal book, What Makes a Champion! in 2002. Championship in the broadest sense of the word—being the best that you can be in all aspects of your life—is a quality that we too have been interested in since the late nineties, and our collaboration with Professor Snyder has enabled strategies for inculcating the Champion Mindset in young people."

David and Brian add that Professor Snyder, coined the term "Champion Mindset" and that it was he who observed, "In the best of times the Champion Mindset is a valuable commodity; in the worst of times it is an absolute necessity."

At a personal level, a Champion Mindset has fueled David Chiem's life success and leadership. It has also enhanced his commitment to learning. Let's explore how a desire to learn enables a person to be the best that they can be (particularly, when being the best involves outstanding leadership).

Leadership is Learning

A number of studies show that exceptional leaders achieve their potential through the pursuit of learning, knowledge, and wisdom. Taking the time to read this book indicates your learning mind is engaged and active.

In a whitepaper titled, "Expectations Create Outcomes: Growth Mindsets in Organizations," Chris Miller, the program director at University of North Carolina Executive Development, reports leaders with a learning mindset:

- "Actively seek ways to improve;
- Surround themselves with able and talented people because they are not threatened by them;
- Admit their mistakes and learn from them;
- Forecast the skills they and their teams will need in the future…;
- Ask for feedback because it is seen as a learning opportunity …, and
- Reward efforts and not only outcomes…"

Miller's conclusion can be summarized in three words: leaders are learners.

According to Miller, by engaging a learning mindset a leader also fosters curiosity and learning effectiveness among their team members. This, in turn, can impact a business's "culture and employee productivity. It can also improve employee motivation, retention, and loyalty, and can spur collaboration, innovation, and creative problem solving at all organizational levels." In chapter three, you will see how David Chiem's insatiable pursuit of wisdom and personal growth are reflected in MindChamps' core values and culture. Later in this chapter, you will learn how David's pursuit of learning led him into acting and film production which opened him up to the importance of creativity and innovation in the context of his personal life and business. David's penchant for creativity, theater, and storytelling align well with a burgeoning field of research linking creativity to leadership success.

Links between Creativity and Leadership

In an article titled, "Creativity and the Role of the Leader," published in the **Harvard Business Review**, Harvard Business school professors Teresa Amabile and Multi Khaire describe how creativity has been an undervalued leadership trait:

> "Creativity has always been at the heart of business, but until now it hasn't been at the top of the management agenda… creativity is essential to the entrepreneurship that gets new businesses started and that sustains the best companies after they have reached global scale. But perhaps because creativity was considered unmanageable—too elusive and intangible to pin down—or because concentrating on it produced a less immediate payoff than improving

execution, it hasn't been the focus of most managers' attention.

Despite a history of companies underappreciating leadership creativity, in a 2018 article for Clutch, Lysa Miller—President and Founder of the MetroWest Women's Network —cites research from IBM which "found that creativity was ranked the most important leadership quality for success in business, outweighing integrity and global thinking. There are many advantages to creative leadership within companies, including:

- Problem solving
- Achieving growth
- Mentoring teams in the workplace
- Finding unlikely perspectives within the business."

This research, and other studies like it, highlights the importance of developing creative strengths in the context of life and business stewardship. It also suggests the importance of leveraging imagination to creatively solve human problems.

Leadership experts like Professor James Kouzes and Professor Barry Posner (both from Santa Clara University), have dedicated their careers to studying what makes an outstanding leader. In their book **The Leadership Challenge: How to Make Extraordinary Things Happen in Organizations**, these men define five practices that make a leader exceptional. One of those five practices involves translating imagination into creative solutions that resolve important customer or social needs. Specifically, Professor Kouzes and Professor Posner note, "Leaders envision the future by imagining exciting and ennobling possibilities. You need to make something happen, to change the way things are, to create something that no one else has ever created before."

MindChamps' success is inextricably linked to David Chiem's mindset which seeks and encourages mastery, learning, and creativity. Without further ado, let's open our minds to learn about Mr. David Chiem, Founder, CEO, and Executive Chairman of MindChamps.

David Chiem–Leadership Born of Adversity and Triumph

Ms. Helen Keller, the first person who was blind and deaf to earn a Bachelor of Arts degree, said, "Character cannot be developed in ease and quiet. Only through experience of trial and suffering can the soul be strengthened, ambition inspired, and success achieved." Those words were true for Ms. Keller and equally true for Mr. David Chiem.

In my view, the seeds of David's leadership were sown in his youth and his future successes could have been predicted based on his response to early childhood adversity (his Champion mindset). To fully understand David's journey, let's reflect back to the days preceding the fall of Saigon in 1975.

As United States troops pulled out of Vietnam at the end of the war, thousands of South Vietnamese and families of military leaders were helicoptered to safety onto five U.S. aircraft carriers. Many others, like David's family, were not as lucky.

His parents had operated a provision shop and resided in a four-storey home. David picks up the story by noting, "I remember in 1975, I was on the ground playing when I was overshadowed by two men. They abruptly asked if they were at the home of Chiem. Little did I know that when I said yes, they would arrest my father."

CHAPTER TWO

David shared that his mother worked feverishly for the next year to secure his father's release.

The fall of Saigon would mark a mass exodus from Vietnam that took place over the next five years. Estimates of those fleeing the country vary. The number successfully arriving to seek asylum in various countries is generally put at between 650,000 and 800,000, but the number originally setting out on the one-way journey is reputed to be up to double this number. The attrition rate was enormous, but for many families, a chance at a new beginning and a better future for their children was an imperative.

David's family lived in the Vietnamese city of Rach Gia. In his book titled **Cuc: Flower of the Delta**, journalist Mr. Peter Geniesse notes, "Rach Gia in mid-1978 was the home of 'Rust Bucket Tours, Inc.'…the tag given to the capital of Kien Giang Province by American refugee relief workers. The city was a long way from Saigon, but it was situated on the Gulf of Thailand, convenient to Malaysia and Indonesia as well as Thailand…Rach Gia…had become the major center for escape from the country.' David, his parents, and his two older siblings escaped by making it onto one of the tiny and dangerously overcrowded fishing boats, which carried desperate families across the treacherous South China Sea.

David's family arrived in Malaysia's Pulau Bidong, where they lived in a refugee camp. David was nine-years-old and living conditions were bleak in the camp. Four months into their stay, David's mother snuck out of the camp to pawn what little she had in order to secure money for the family's basic needs.

With good fortune, the day after David's mother made her desperate excursion from the camp, his family learned that the Australian government had randomly selected them for asylum.

Against this challenging backdrop, he committed himself to overcome adversity. David shared, "I learned early that a person's mindset is essential to survival and success. My father encouraged me to strive and set myself apart. He said that this was our rebirth; that for every one of us who made it to Australia, someone else had died. This taught me not to take anything for granted – including life itself."

While David's story vastly improved upon his arrival in Australia, his entire family faced considerable transitional challenges. Specifically, he recalls being unable to respond to questions posed to him in school because he couldn't speak English. He recounts episodes of name calling and other painful experiences not uncommon among young immigrants. David notes, "My father helped me respond to my challenges by emphasizing the importance of learning. He reminded me that of all the things we lost back in Vietnam, one thing people can never take from you is what you learn. That nurtured me on my course as a life-long learner."

Armed with his hunger for learning, David excelled at school, and although his family's expectation was for him to enter medicine, by age 14, David had already developed a passion for the world of the Arts and, in particular, creative expression through story-telling. In 1984, he was the "first Asian to win a lead role on mainstream Australian television", in a drama series titled Butterfly Island. From there, David's creative and educational pursuits led him to study the craft of acting at the Theatre Nepean. He went on to lead roles in television, theatre, film, and radio. He graduated with a Bachelor of Arts in Communication from the University of Technology, Sydney, and completed a post-graduate Producer's Specialist year at the prestigious Australian Film, Television and Radio School (AFTRS). These academic accomplishments reflect persistence, a desire to rise above the ordinary, a quest for knowledge, and the development of creative skills.

David's early life journey reflects, in Helen Keller's words, character born from trial and suffering. His life accomplishments, including the success of MindChamps, reflect resourcefulness, adaptivity, determination, and above all else, the mindset of a champion, a learner, and a creative person. His curiosity transferred to an unrelenting interest in learning and education. That curiosity prompted him to create ways to integrate his background in the arts with leaders in education and science, pursuing a visionary approach to improving the way children learn and grow. His journey and his mindset offer lessons to all current and aspiring leaders.

Partnering Along the Journey

While the world of education tends to operate in 'silos', what makes the MindChamps approach both unique and revolutionary, is that it is able to synthesize research and insights from the four distinct domains of Education, Neuroscience, Psychology and Theater. This is due in no small part to its drive to connect with world-leaders in their disciplines — and to David Chiem's unique ability to communicate the power of his vision to people whose passions dove-tail perfectly with the MindChamps Way. These are people whose dedication to their work cannot be purchased — whose respect and collaboration must be earned — and their contribution to the MindChamps ethos is palpable.

In a 2017 *Straits Times* article, David told reporter Wong

Kim Hoh, "When I first started, people laughed at me and said: 'Governments spend billions on education every year. Who are you to start a global approach to education?' With the resilience and persistence of a growth-oriented champion, he forged on and according to the Straits Times, soon after setting up MindChamps, he had a breakthrough when he met Professor Allan Snyder... As he remembers it, "It took three years to win his trust." Now, Professor Snyder is MindChamps' Chair of Research.

In their book, **The 3-Mind Revolution**, David Chiem and Brian Caswell highlight how MindChamps benefitted from Professor Snyder's research conducted at the University of Sydney and the Australian National University, noting, "The Centre for the Mind was the brainchild of Emeritus Professor Allan Snyder—a groundbreaking Marconi-Award-winning researcher, acknowledged as one of the most innovative scientific thinkers of the past 50 years. A Fellow of the Royal Society, he is a man who has made breakthroughs in three different fields and we are proud to have collaborated with him, to give his pioneering research practical application in the world of education."

In addition to Professor Snyder, David and MindChamps' leaders leverage on guidance from the MindChamps World Research, Advisory & Education Team. This group consists of diverse renowned contributors. Let's take a moment to briefly review backgrounds for some of these advisors, realizing that space will not allow for a full description of credentials of everyone who offers MindChamps their expertise. As such, I will highlight the background of MindChamps' most senior advisors and summarize some of the accomplishments of the organization's advisory fellows and senior fellows.

CHAPTER TWO

The name Brian Caswell is likely familiar by now given my repeated mentions of him in the context of his work with David. Brian is MindChamps' Dean of Research and Programme Development. His influence on MindChamps has been foundational and profound. Brian has had a lifelong love for both reading and writing. He has authored more than 200 books, received numerous literary awards, and has been appointed to the Australia Council Literature Board's Register of Peers. Brian has spent much of his career studying the neuroscience of learning and the psychology related to the development of the learning mind.

One reason for the productive chemistry which exists between David and Brian is the fact that, even before the inception of MindChamps, they had already developed a deep, creative rapport, as co-authors of award-winning fiction books such as **Only the Heart** and **The Full Story**. They have also written successful non-fiction childhood education books such as **The 3-Mind Revolution: The New World View for Global Leaders, Educators, and Parents; Deeper than the Ocean; Pre-school Parenting Secrets: Talking with the Sky** and **The Art of Communicating with Your Child**.

Brian Caswell has over 40 years' experience in private and public education and shares that knowledge not only through his role as MindChamps' Dean of Research and Programme Development but also as a speaker and literacy consultant.

Professor Kathy Hirsh-Pasek (a senior fellow at the Brookings Institute and the Director of the Infant Language Laboratory at Temple University) and **Professor Roberta Michnick Golinkoff** (Director of the Child's Play, Learning and Development Laboratory at the University of Delaware), are international authorities on early childhood development and language acquisition and are in great demand around the world for their insight and their innovative approach to curriculum design. They are the authors of numerous papers and the 'must-read' books, Einstein *Never Used Flashcards* and *Becoming Brilliant – What Science Tells Us About Raising Successful Children.*

MindChamps' Dean of Music in Education is **Professor Larry Scripp**. Professor Scripp is a founding Chair in the Music Education Department at Boston University's New England Conservatory. He has researched children's artistic development and assessed arts and education programs as part of Harvard University's Project Zero. Professor Scripp is also a highly-regarded music director, composer, and musician.

Mr. Steven Andrews, a former senior education advisor to the British government during the Tony Blair administration, serves as MindChamps' Chief Academic Officer. He has also served as the Director of Schools in Greenwich, England, and the Group Chief Education Officer for Cognita International Schools.

Dr. Scott Hicks (Academy Award Nominee and Emmy Award-winning screenwriter and director) is the director of *Shine; Snow Falling on Cedars; Hearts in Atlantis; No Reservations* and numerous other critically-acclaimed films. His deep understanding of the creative process from a theoretical and a practical stand-point is an invaluable asset to the organization in its drive to develop aspects of the Creative Mind.

Bringing more than 35-years' experience from the Singapore School system, **Mrs. Carmee Lim**—MindChamps' Mentor Principal—was also the Principal of one of Singapore's premier schools, the Raffles Girls' School. Mrs. Lim has also been the Senior

CHAPTER TWO

Inspector of Schools in the Ministry of Education and the First Executive Director of the Academy of Principles in Singapore.

Mrs. Louise Mulligan-Andrews serves as MindChamps' Director General of Education. Mrs. Mulligan-Andrews was the former director of schools for the United Kingdom's Department of Education. She also helped improve student exam performance to double the national rate in Nottingham City (England's midland region).

Mr. Aubrey Mellor (Former director of Australia's National Institute of Dramatic Arts and recipient of the Order of Australia Medal) is one of Australia's most renowned theater teachers and directors. His lifetime of experience in theater and his mastery of theatrical strategies has been a boon in the development of the MindChamps theater-based education strategies.

Professor Trevor Cairney is Adjunct Professor at the University of New South Wales, and a recipient of the Order of Australia Medal. He is an expert in early-childhood literacy-development and has had a stellar academic career in both the academic world (Dean of Education and Pro-Vice-Chancellor, University of Western Sydney; Director, Centre for Regional Research and Innovation; University Life Professorial Fellow, University of NSW, Australia).

Ms. Libby Gleeson is a beloved, multi-award-winning children's author and Adjunct Associate Professor at the University of Sydney, Department of Education and Social Work. She is also Chair of WestWords, Western Sydney's Literature Development Organization for Young People. Her lifetime of service to children's literature and literacy makes her an ideal collaborator in the development of MindChamps multiple literacies approach.

Mr. Dean Carey serves as the Dean of Theater at MindChamps. Among his many credits and roles, Mr. Carey has been the CEO and Founding Director of Actors Centre Australia, and the Former Head of Acting at the Western Australian Academy of Performing Arts (WAPA) and the National Institute of Dramatic Arts (NIDA). Mr. Carey has also personally coached prominent stage and A-List Hollywood actors such as Hugh Jackman and has consulted extensively for theater and television productions.

While the list of credentials for this esteemed advisory board is impressive, their collective expertise can only add value to MindChamps if the company's leaders seek guidance from them. As you might expect from my description of David's commitment to personal learning and growth, he has not let this advisory body sit idle. These experts are routinely asked for input and they regularly meet at MindChamps' Headquarters in Singapore. Among other things, their meetings serve to update the MindChamps curriculum development and training teams on innovations related to education.

It's noble for MindChamps leaders to invite the input of these experts, but do they listen to them and incorporate their insights into operational, process, or curriculum improvements? During a 2018 visit, advisory team member and MindChamps Dean of Music Dr. Larry Scripp reflected on the dynamic exchanges that take place during these advisory meetings. "MindChamps is the first educational organization that I have encountered that believes in and builds on empirical research in education… That's why I decided to join MindChamps. It is a perfect marriage of theory and practice in education, and a better understanding of what 21st Century education can be."

CHAPTER TWO

In addition to engaging in dialogues with the MindChamps World Research Advisory & Education Team designed to shape learning for the 21st Century, MindChamps leaders are also invited to host global forums like the major event held in Beijing's National Olympic Stadium (also referred to as the Bird's Nest) entitled, "**The 3-Mind Movement: Education for the Future Symposium**".

Over 200 experts in global learning and representatives from child education organizations participated in the symposium, which was also broadcast through live-streaming nation-wide. The event received news coverage on the People's Republic of China's state television and various other media sources.

While there are thousands of education organizations in the field, MindChamps has distinguished itself thanks to its core DNA. As David puts it, "Unlike other products, education should not be treated as a matter of personal preference. Children's minds are too precious to be left to individual opinion, and their nurturing and care must be based on the latest and best empirical research available."

The 2018 event also saw the launch of the Chinese language version of David and Brian's book, **The 3-Mind Revolution** by the Beijing Institute of Technology Press, one of China's most prominent publishers – in essence, opening up to more than 1.2 billion Chinese speaking people their ideas regarding the urgency of early childhood education reform.

MindChamps: The Outgrowth of a Champion's Mind

By now, there should be little doubt that MindChamps springs from a man with a champion, learning, and creative mind. David

Chiem overcame childhood adversity, maintained optimism, and stoked a hunger for learning. He also developed his creative craft and established a vision to transform and revolutionize education.

Despite a chorus of cynics who suggested he would never realize his dream, David redoubled his efforts and creatively partnered with experts to 'take on the Goliath of the education system', beat the odds and launch MindChamps. It is with that same willingness to dream big, partner well, and work hard, that he continues to advance MindChamps on its rapid growth path.

In an interview following his award as 'Top 10 CEO' in 2014, David was asked to name the biggest challenge he has had to overcome. His reply was enlightening. "The biggest challenge," he said, "is to get people to believe in you, when you have nothing." For over two decades, MindChamps has managed against all odds to maintain its clarity and purpose, and this can be attributed to David's ability to remain focused on the mission, vision, charter, values, and core themes of the organization. We will now look at these key elements which serve as the inspiration and the engine behind **The MindChamps Way**.

CHAPTER TWO

Follow the Red Dot

- Consider the openness or fixed nature of your mindset. How would you rate your champion, learning, and creative mind? What opportunities do you have to develop skills in support of each?
- Think about what you are doing and can do to foster a growth mindset in your home or more broadly in the lives of children, so they develop "the tools to succeed in their pursuits."
- Reflecting on how you lead others, to what degree do you actively seek ways to improve, surround yourself with able and talented people, and admit your mistakes? What area offers you the greatest growth opportunity?
- How are you exercising your creativity? In what ways are you encouraging others to do the same?
- How would you describe your ability to "envision the future by imagining exciting and ennobling possibilities?" How would others describe you in this regard?
- Consider how "trial and suffering" have strengthened your soul, inspired your ambition, and helped you achieve success.
- How would you assess your overall commitment to learning? What can you point to in support of your assessment?
- Which thought leaders and experts do you seek out for guidance? How regularly do you seek their input? In what ways have you used their input to drive improvements?
- How can you, in the words of Mr. Steve Jobs (echoed by Mr. David Chiem's example), "start small, think big…Put a ding in the universe."?

CHAPTER THREE

From Purpose to Culture

Vision without action is merely a dream.
Action without vision just passes the time.
Vision with action can change the world.

Joel Barker
Author, Technology, and Business Futurist

In chapter two, we discussed how David Chiem's vision to revolutionize education is becoming a global reality. In this chapter, we will examine how he has effectively shared his vision and infused it purposefully into the MindChamps culture. A colleague of mine, leadership speaker and psychologist Dr. Terry Paulson, notes that the difference between leadership "vision and a hallucination is how many people see it." In other words, if you are the only one in your organization following your leadership vision, you are hallucinating. In the pages that follow, you will experience how David's vision has been effectively shared, "seen," and mobilized throughout MindChamps.

This chapter's title, "**From Purpose to Culture**," highlights the importance of communicating a clear vision and assuring that vision guides daily action. As part of our exploration, we will first review the role leaders play in culture development. Additionally, we will address the importance of orientation, training, and management systems in the creation of a rich business culture.

After offering an overview of core concepts, you will see how MindChamps has articulated its mission, vision, social charter, values, and core themes. You will also peek into processes by which MindChamps leaders drive their cultural tenets through interactions with one another, team members, business partners, teachers, family members, students, and all other stakeholders.

Having been an organizational consultant for close to 30 years, I have experienced some rather remarkable leaders and corporate cultures. My time inside corporate offices at Starbucks, Mercedes-Benz, Godiva, Pandora Jewelry, The Ritz-Carlton Hotel Company, and many others have provided me with ample opportunities to work alongside extraordinary visionaries. I've also experienced how vibrant and vital workplace cultures have given my clients a competitive advantage. As a result of a differentiated corporate culture, I've seen firsthand how companies achieve enhanced growth and profitability—not unlike that of MindChamps.

Emeritus Harvard University Leadership Professor John Kotter and Emeritus Harvard University Professor of Business Logistics James Heskett, spent four years conducting studies that looked at the relationship between business success and corporate culture. These researchers then shared their findings in the book *Corporate Culture and Performance*. According to Kotter and Heskett, their four key findings were:

> "Corporate culture can have a significant impact on a firm's long-term economic performance…

CHAPTER THREE

> Corporate culture will probably be an even more important factor in determining the success or failure of firms in the next decade…
>
> Corporate cultures that inhibit strong long-term financial performance are not rare; they develop easily, even in firms that are full of reasonable and intelligent people…
>
> Although tough to change, corporate cultures can be made more performance enhancing…"

In one study, Kotter and Heskett found that over an eleven-year period, companies that effectively engaged employees, customers, and stockholders substantially out-performed those that did not. These differences were seen in revenue increases (stronger cultures showing a 682% increase compared to 166% for businesses with weaker cultures), work force expansion (282% for strong culture vs. 36% for weak), stock price (901% as opposed to 74%) and net income growth (756% vs. 1%). Need I say more?

Before we dive into the clarity of MindChamps' purposeful vision and the strength of culture at MindChamps, let's take a moment to align on a common understanding for terms like vision, mission, and culture.

The Why and How of Business

From my vantage point, running a business without clearly defining a company's vision, mission, and values is like taking your family on a long trip without knowing your destination, the purpose of your travel, or having navigational tools such as a map or GPS. You will end up somewhere, it might even work out well—but there will be a lot of uncertainty, angst, and meandering along the way. J.R.R. Tolkien wrote, "Not all those who wander are lost." However, I've seen my share of "lost" leaders who have let their companies wander without the tools needed to achieve. That is certainly not the case at MindChamps!

Three tools required for a company to reach its potential are a company vision, a mission statement, and clearly-defined values. These tools are interrelated, distinctly important, and often misunderstood by business leaders. Let's quickly explore each, so you can appreciate the elegance of these cultural components at MindChamps.

Vision/Mission/Values

Any discussion of vision, mission, and values must come with a strong caveat. Leadership thinkers and consultants have long debated the meaning of each of these terms and those debates have led to a lot of confusion across the business landscape. For example, imagine you are looking at the mission statement and corporate vision of two similar companies. We will call them Business A and Business B. It's not unusual for Business A's mission statement to read like Business B's corporate vision and vice a versa. To help steer past this confusion, I'll provide distinctions between a corporate vision statement and a mission statement that reflect consensus among colleagues. These distinctions have also proven to be effective for my clients. Enough of the disclaimers and on to the definitions.

Vision versus Mission – The concept of a leadership vision has likely been with us since the dawn of time. Fifth-century BC Athenian general and historian Thucydides purportedly declared,

CHAPTER THREE

"The bravest are surely those who have the clearest vision of what is before them, glory and danger alike, and yet notwithstanding, go out to meet it." Unfortunately, many leaders haven't taken the time to define their vision. Others have hastily written out a vision because they knew they were expected to have one.

In my book, **The Zappos Experience**, I profile an American online retailer Zappos.com. Much like MindChamps, Zappos was an outgrowth of its visionary CEO Tony. Also, like MindChamps, Zappos grew quickly and exponentially. Zappos was launched in 1999 and was purchased ten years later by Amazon.com for $1.2 billion. A pivotal moment in Zappos' success journey occurred when Tony Hsieh overcame his resistance to writing down a leadership vision. I capture that moment in my book, noting, "Early on, although some aspects of the Zappos key business values were being articulated publicly, none had been codified into a...document. Like many entrepreneurs, the early leaders at Zappos were doers. They saw opportunity and seized it. By nature, they sought to be nimble and adaptive and did not wish to be encumbered by policies and practices associated with corporate behemoths." I go on to note that Zappos' leadership resisted producing a written vision (and related cultural guideposts), as "they viewed the document production process as a fundamentally 'corporate exercise.' However, in the end, scalability and the unsettling nature of growth pushed the company to translate its unique culture into words." You will see later in this chapter that David was never reluctant to share his vision, mission, or values. MindChamps' leadership also took the steps needed to craft and share those important concepts.

From my perspective, a company's vision should reflect the "ideal world" that leaders seek to nurture or create. In essence, a vision statement expresses a dream of a better tomorrow. It should be an aspiration that inspires team members. Well-crafted vision statements are clear, concise, and memorable. Here are a few excellent corporate and non-profit examples of a defined vision:

Alzheimer's Association: A world without Alzheimer's.
Amazon: To be earth's most customer-centric company…
Oxfam: A just world without poverty.
The Nature Conservancy: To leave a sustainable world for future generations.
Mercedes-Benz USA: To be dedicated to customers and driven by excellence.
Pandora Jewelry: To be the branded manufacturer that delivers the most personal jewelry experience.
Zappos: Delivering happiness to customers, employees, and vendors.

In our upcoming discussion of MindChamps' vision statement, you will see that it meets all four essential criteria. It is clear, concise, inspirational, and memorable.

While a company's vision statement expresses an "ideal world," an organization's mission statement should share why a company exists. That why statement must define how an organization is capable of advancing the world in the direction of the company's vision. Like a corporate vision, a mission statement should be concise.

The Society for Human Resource Managers aptly describes the linkage between a mission statement and an organization's vision by noting, "A mission statement is a concise explanation of the organization's reason for existence. It describes the organization's purpose and its overall intention. The mission statement supports the vision and serves to communicate purpose and direction to employees, customers, vendors and other stakeholders."

Rather than listing a series of outstanding mission statements, I will tender only one example, so we can expeditiously get to the cultural infrastructure of MindChamps. That example is reflected in Apple's mission under the leadership of Steve Jobs. That statement reads, "To make a contribution to the world by making tools for the mind that advance humankind." That version of Apple's mission communicated why Apple came to be.

In his book, **Start with Why: How Great Leaders Inspire Everyone to Take Action**, Simon Sinek suggests that Apple's uniqueness "was not their ability to build such a fast-growth company. It wasn't their ability to think differently about personal computers. What has made Apple special is that they've been able to repeat the pattern over and over and over. …Apple has successfully challenged conventional thinking with the computer industry, the small electronics industry, the music industry, the mobile phone industry and the broader entertainment industry. And the reason is simple. Apple inspires. Apple starts with Why."

It's time to look at how MindChamps starts with their why, and how leaders at MindChamps link their why or mission statement to the company's vision. In the process of exploring these topics, we will also discuss MindChamps' value structure and how MindChamps' leaders drive alignment with core elements of their culture.

Our Calling and Corporate DNA

When you click on the MindChamps.org website, the first header tab you will see is titled "About Us," and the first option on that tab is titled "Our Calling and Corporate DNA." The prominence of the information housed on the "Our Calling and Corporate DNA" page speaks to how leaders prioritize culture at MindChamps. Many brands are unwilling to publicly post mission, vision, values, and other elements of culture—as if they were afraid that they might someday be held accountable to them. The inverse is true for MindChamps!

Every elemental component of MindChamps culture is proudly and prominently displayed and placed in context by a welcome message from David Chiem. In his opening remarks, David sets the context for how MindChamps seeks to be of service to all of its stakeholders. His thoughts set a framework for MindChamps vision, mission, and values anchored to MindChamps commitment to unleash the full potential of every child. In David's words:

> "Are some people simply born to succeed, while others are born to fail?' Science says 'No!' As human beings, the ability to learn and grow is encoded in our DNA. We have a virtually infinite potential for success.
>
> Of course, when it comes to our DNA, what turns the potential into the actual is the quality of our experiences – especially in the first 15 years of life. Our DNA provides the potential, but it is our experiences that release that potential, to shape it, focus it and hopefully, turn it into what the world recognizes as success.

CHAPTER THREE

MindChamps was founded almost two decades ago, on the belief that if we understand how we learn, we can find the best ways of targeting and releasing the potential in every child.

MindChamps is constantly researching ways to liberate and train the instinct for creativity and problem-solving that is encoded into the DNA of all our young champs."

In a video that appears below David's greeting, viewers clearly appreciate that "MindChamps began as a calling—a calling to make a difference to create an approach to education in tune with the demands of a rapidly changing world." That calling is at the center of MindChamps' Vision and Mission—which are also displayed on that highly prominent orientation webpage.

MindChamps defines its vision succinctly, engagingly, and inspirationally. MindChamps' ideal state is presented in eleven impactful words:

To nurture the power of human potential for a better tomorrow.

To make that vision a possibility, MindChamps defines its why as a mission to:

...challenge and improve education standards globally.

Putting these statements together, MindChamps exists **to challenge and improve education standards globally**, in pursuit of a world where the **power of human potential creates a better tomorrow**.

It is quite evident that MindChamps is operating from world-class culture objectives! Moreover, given the prominent display of these cultural tenets, (in the words of Simon Sinek), MindChamps starts with their "why."

In Order to Achieve Your Mission, You Must Be Values Based

Mr. Jack Welch, former chairman and CEO of General Electric, observed that when it comes to vision and culture, "Good business leaders create a vision, articulate the vision, passionately own the vision, and relentlessly drive it to completion." Part of the relentless drive needed to achieve one's mission involves defining the values which should shape decisions and action.

Early in MindChamps' evolution, the company's leaders carved out several ways to identify five core values that would guide the future of the business. David Chiem shares, "If our business were a tree, we knew our values would be the roots. They would hold us in place and nurture our daily course. We knew we had to get them right because they would be our perpetual anchors and as is the case with roots, they would be underground and couldn't be touched. We operate from the same values we defined more than 20 years ago. As such, we engaged in robust debate and it was quite challenging to get them down to a manageable set. Once we identified our five core values, we went through the process of prioritizing them."

CHAPTER THREE

MindChamps defines its five core values as:
- *Heart*
- *Integrity*
- *Prosperity*
- *Growth*
- *Expansion*

David goes on to explain how each value was ranked. "Heart and Integrity both moved to the top of our lists quickly. There was lengthy discussion with some leaders saying that placing heart as the primary value would be unrealistic for a private organization — since outsiders could challenge whether each and every decision was made based on emotional considerations. As we talked about it more, we realized that we had always been committed to making complex decisions that place the best interest of children at the center of everything we do. We live in a complex environment, and the adult world can create a lot of 'fluff' and distraction — placing Heart as the number one value, however, has enabled us to guide all of our decision-making by asking — 'How do we do what is best for each child?'"

David reports that integrity is essential to trust and as such was an obvious second ranking value. He adds, "There was a lot of discussion about prosperity, growth, and expansion. For us, prosperity means more than wealth and money. To prosper means to thrive and we are fully committed to assuring that all stakeholders thrive." With regard to the MindChamps growth value, David suggests, "Growth is more than growing as a business. It is fully aligned with a learning mindset. It specifically addresses personal growth and attaining our own personal potential. At MindChamps, we foster champion potential. To do that, we must never stop growing. We must love growth and the process of growing. Finally, expansion is essential for us to realize our mission. We are not here to serve a single community. We are here to serve the global community. We are also not just here to serve our present generation. We want to create a movement that serves generation after generation."

Creating a 'Fun' Environment

David notes, "The values were there from the beginning, but in 2002, when we were establishing the Singapore HQ, we were faced with an important question. Many organizations talk about creating a worker-friendly or a fun environment, but how do you sustain that fun environment when there are so many daily pressures and KPIs that must be met? We realized that 'fun' is not built from a series of ad hoc moments — that to maintain it as a culture, we needed to craft a workplace environment that was satisfying and emotionally sustaining, so we devised six themes designed to structure an environment that would sustain the fun. We use the anagram C.R.E.A.T.E. to encapsulate these themes."

That anagram represents the following themes:
- Consistency
- Realistic
- Excellence
- Accountability
- Teamwork and
- Energy.

CHAPTER THREE

As David explains them, "Consistency must exist at all levels, from the cleaner to the CEO. If a team-member drops the ball once or twice, someone will help pick it up, but if the same thing keeps happening, the fun disappears rapidly for everyone.

"Being realistic when setting goals and tasks is important. It is essential to set ambitious goals for every department, but self-worth and job-satisfaction derive from achieving our goals and it is no fun if the goal is totally unrealistic and never achieved.

"Excellence at MindChamps is about delivering the highest of standards to our full potential, but it is not necessarily about being perfect. Rather, it asks the question, 'What do we do about it?' when something is not going right and addressing it immediately. How we deal with missteps and failures and what we learn from them is what creates excellence, and if we work from this perspective, we remove unwanted pressure and free up the capacity of team-members to push the boundaries and think outside the square.

"The word 'Accountability' sounds like the opposite of fun, but that is because it has always been associated with an external pressure to perform. Accountability, in the MindChamps sense, is defined as, 'taking 100% responsibility personally for all our actions'. Linking to our philosophy of Excellence, if the environment encourages and rewards self-assessment and discourages blame and judgment, every team-member is empowered because energy and creativity is sapped by blame and the emotions associated with it — and that is no fun. Encouraging personal accountability embraces this concept and fosters a deeper engagement in day to day activities.

"In the world of motivational speakers, the word TEAM is

represented as 'Together, Everyone Achieves More'. Of course, more people working together on a task should be able to achieve more, however, for us at MindChamps, if we are truly working together, we don't simply achieve more — we achieve 'Miracles'."

Hold on. Did he just say 'miracles'?

I've been a consultant in business for almost three decades and most leaders would regard the notion of a miracle as new-age and vague with no place in their corporate thinking — but for David Chiem the notion is as tangible as a spread-sheet or a P&L statement.

As he explains it, "I've said previously that it took perhaps three years to win the trust of Allan Snyder. I recall the moment when Allan agreed to become a part of MindChamps. He gave me a big hug, and said, 'David, if two people — just two people — can trust each other 100%, they can change the world.' True Teamwork is about creating deep trust, unshackled by the fear of judgment. It is only when this occurs that we can make the breakthroughs that no one believed possible — and that, not some 'new-age' notion of magic, is the real definition of a miracle."

Energy, the final MindChamps theme, David explains in this way.

"Coming from a theater background, one of the things I quickly learned was the concept of Energy. We can either create or sap energy in the people around us. A leader's number one duty is to create energy — or, at minimum to protect it — because an environment that is is 'energy-sapping' definitely no fun. Leaders need to observe their own energy and that of individual team-members. Energy is involved in everything we do, everything we say and everything we project."

CHAPTER THREE

Before I shift from this conceptual discussion to a review of the ways MindChamps' leaders seek to operationalize these important cultural components, I must share an additional feature of MindChamps' cultural declaration. It is one that is far too often disregarded by leaders — MindChamps' social charter.

As you likely know, social charters date back centuries. They usually were agreements forged between countries or between a government and its citizens. Commonstrust.org defines a social charter as a way to help "operationalize the interests and practices of a(n)…association of stakeholders…It is a written framework which outlines the rights and incentives of a community for the management and protection of its common resources." When created in the context of business, a social charter typically signals a company's corporate responsibility. Social charters in a business context are declarations of how a company seeks to "do good" in the world. It also guides employees, vendors, and other business partners toward socially responsible action. In the case of MindChamps, their public facing social charter reads:

Education Enables
__MindChamps is committed to the creation of educational opportunities where they would not otherwise exist.__

MindChamps' social charter makes it clear that leaders seek to "create educational opportunities" for those in need and expect its business partners and team members to join with them in the fulfillment of that commitment.

Branding with Culture in Mind

An organization's branding should both reflect and influence the wider perception, in the minds of the public, of what that organization stands for and what it promises.

Ms. Michelle Peh is MindChamps' Group General Manager and Chief Brand Officer — and the fact that both roles are combined says a lot about the importance of branding in the MindChamps ethos.

She shares, "At MindChamps, branding is not just about clever advertising or glossy marketing collaterals. It is an externalized expression of the soul of the organization. It encapsulates the way we live and breathe the MindChamps principles and values as a team.

"In summary, the brand personality of a MindChampion is someone who possesses the 3 Minds in perfect balance and faces life with 100% Respect and Zero Fear.

"A MindChampion is someone who can believe in, and live, the following 10 aspirational statements:

- I am Creative
- I am Compassionate
- I am a Life-Long Learner
- I am Confident
- I am Grateful
- I have Integrity
- I am Self-Reflective
- I Focus on the Beauty in Others
- I Embrace Setbacks as Setups
- I Value Feedback as a Seed for Growth

CHAPTER THREE

"These values are inculcated throughout the PreSchool curriculum and appear prominently on the PreSchool branding collaterals — but they are promoted throughout the organization, as well. In fact, to connect all team members, we created a special culture statement:

"One Heart, Connected Minds, Nurturing MindChampions."

Entrepreneur Nolan Bushnell, the founder of more than 20 companies including Chuck E. Cheese and Atari observed, "A lot of people have ideas, but there are few who decide to do something about them now. Not tomorrow. Not next week. But today. The true entrepreneur is a doer, not a dreamer." When it comes to culture, words and ideas must be supported by action. As such, let's look at actions built into the MindChamps operational structure in support of the company's mission, vision, values, themes, and social charter.

Culture in Action

In my book about Zappos, I titled one of my chapters "Culture Should Be A Verb," signifying that culture is not a destination or an aspiration. It is a way of being and it lives in a business' day-to-day operation.

Since MindChamps runs its own centers and supports franchise partners, leaders at MindChamps work to assure that its internal culture is also reflected in the operation of centers run throughout the franchise community. Given the scope of the MindChamps brand, let's first look at an example of how MindChamps' leaders foster culture for their corporate team and then look at how they drive extraordinary culture alignment with their franchise partners.

David shares, "Our corporate team gets together every other month and we celebrate our values at every meeting. That celebration involves multi-disciplinary teams such as marketing and finance coming together to create a unique presentation of our featured value. Each brief presentation strengthens teamwork. The groups rate one another on creativity and how well they express the value. Given the frequency of our meetings, we continually reinforce our values and help new team members engage creatively and collaboratively to bring them to life."

The exponential growth of MindChamps is a reflection of how effectively MindChamps' values are being translated into action across corporately owned centers. As writer, consultant, and speaker, Dennis Whately observes, "The results you achieve will be in direct proportion to the effort you apply." MindChamps corporate team members are applying considerable effort to live the company's values.

MindChamps leaders also invest heavily to foster the MindChamps culture (as well as educational quality and operational excellence) across all franchise operations. In chapter five, you will see the sophisticated management system MindChamps uses to train, support, and grow talent (referred to as the MindChamps ChampionGold Standard) across all centers bearing the MindChamps name. Without getting too far ahead of ourselves, suffice it to say that "Culture and Relationships" represent one of three fundamental aspects of excellence covered by the MindChamps ChampionGold Standard.

MindChamps offers specific culture standards for each center and provides training, resources, and tools to assure alignment and success. The following overview exemplifies how MindChamps introduces cultural expectations as part of their overall management system:

"LEADING CULTURE AND RELATIONSHIPS
Leaders play a crucial role in establishing the unique climate and culture within every MindChamps PreSchool. The culture of the PreSchool, which is a manifestation of the unique MindChamps vision, values, beliefs, and relationships, should be tangible… something which we immediately feel on entry to the PreSchool and which is "lived out" in all aspects of school life.

The PreSchool leader is key to establishing the right organizational conditions for the development of a strong culture and good relationships and is also the prime role model of those relationships and culture.

The ChampionGold leader will lead the culture of the PreSchool in the following key ways:

First Impressions: Develops a school climate, culture, and physical environment which clearly conveys the uniqueness of the MindChamps vision and approach to pre-school education, whilst also ensuring that all receive: 'A Warm Welcome, GREAT learning, and a Fond Farewell'.

'Broadcasting the Vision': Reinforces the culture of the school by consistently modelling, coaching, and 'telling stories' that reinforce the school's mission, vision, values, and norms.

Celebrating Success: Recognizes, celebrates, and communicates the successes of all members of the school community as often and in as many ways as possible.

Cultural Diversity: Builds a climate and learning culture which captures, respects, and celebrates the richness and diversity of the PreSchool family: Champs, parents, and staff.

Engaging Parents and Community: Develops and implements a range of varied and interesting activities to engage parents and the community in the life of the school."

While we will look at MindChamps' global impact in chapter six, I would be remiss not to take a moment (in the context of this discussion of culture) to demonstrate how MindChamps leadership takes action in support of MindChamps' social charter, mission, vision, and values.

Committed to the Creation of Educational Opportunities

As per the MindChamps social charter, leaders have committed "to the creation of educational opportunities where they would not otherwise exist." Also, according to their combined mission and vision statements, those leaders seek "to challenge and improve education standards globally" and "nurture the power of human potential for a better tomorrow." Let's look at the degree to which leadership actions (particularly in the context of philanthropy and social giving) align with their words.

CHAPTER THREE

Even before MindChamps opened the doors to its first PreSchool, the company was demonstrating its commitment to give back. In 2006, for example, MindChamps appointed Jeremy Lim Hon Lee as a Youth Fellow. Jeremy had completed MindChamps Success 4 Life program in 2003.

Jeremy, who suffers from brittle bone disease, was also a Youth Ambassador for the National Kidney Foundation Children's Medical Fund. By 2011, Jeremy had written an autobiography titled **Beyond Bone Breaking**. MindChamps published and launched Jeremy's book (under a spinoff division, MindChamps Publishing). In announcing the book's launch, it was noted that the publication was being released to coincide with Jeremy's 21st birthday. In appreciation for MindChamps' support, Jeremy noted, "I am fortunate to be taught and inspired by my mentor, the founder of MindChamps, Mr. David Chiem and his stable of outstanding teachers. My experiences with them have been rewarding, enriching and life-changing. I have not only learned numerous effective learning methods but also useful life skills that will serve me in my journey through life." The book included a foreword by His Excellency S. R. Nathan, then President of the Republic of Singapore.

Through the years, MindChamps' commitment to create educational opportunities "in places they hadn't previously existed" has produced widespread and substantial economic impact. For example, in 2008, MindChamps provided S$500,000 in scholarships in partnership with the Hong Leong Foundation. The scholarships were "aimed at providing 60 underprivileged neighbourhood school students with innovative learning tools to fully equip them for the upcoming Primary School Leaving Examination (PSLE)."

The scholarship recipients were "chosen from 16 primary schools islandwide" and the students received 13 months of intensive training from MindChamps. While monetary value can be affixed to the cost of the training provided through the scholarships, the life-changing potential of MindChamps training for these recipients is incalculable.

Similarly, MindChamps, working with the Singapore Sports Council, provided complimentary training to athletes who were preparing for Singapore's 2010 Youth Olympic Games. Those athletes participated in a customized offering titled the *MindChamps Youth Athlete 3-Mind Academic Programme*. Three out of seven medals won by Singapore in that Olympic competition went to graduates from that program. One of those medal winners, silver medallist Rainer Ng, shared what MindChamps training meant to him, noting, "MindChamps has given me the courage and determination to break through the negative barriers and beliefs that I have formed over the years. The study techniques I learnt have taught me how to break down and summarize information, making it easier to digest. It has also taught me how to analyse and train smart during my swimming training. I have truly enjoyed every single step of my journey with MindChamps!"

In 2014, MindChamps also partnered with the Toa Payoh East Citizens' Consultative Committee (CCC). That partnership resulted in scholarships which assisted students from underprivileged families living in the Central Singapore District and Bishan-Toa Payoh GRC. Those scholarships, which were named in honor of Mrs. Carmee Lim (MindChamps' Current Mentor Principal), amounted to S$250,000. In reflecting on how the scholarships would help

CHAPTER THREE

deserving students prepare for the PSLE, Mr. Zainudin Nordin, Grassroots Adviser to Bishan-Toa Payoh Grassroots Organisations noted, "This scholarship is about changing lives and improving society. I want to thank MindChamps and Mrs. Carmee Lim for this wonderful idea, to help benefit the needy families in our constituency."

As you can tell, the actions and financial contributions of MindChamps reflect leadership's commitment to improve educational opportunities for those who would not have had access. The behaviour of leadership is also supported and amplified by countless giving acts that come from MindChamps' team members.

I will close this chapter with an extraordinary example of MindChamps' values in action (Heart, Integrity, Prosperity, Growth, and Expansion) demonstrated by MindChamps staff member Dr. William Tan. Dr. Tan is programme mentor of MindChamps Academy. In 2018, Dr. Tan received the Commonwealth Points of Light Award (conferred with a personalized certificate signed by Her Majesty The Queen as Head of the Commonwealth). The prestigious award is given to one volunteer in each of the 52 Commonwealth countries.

In the announcement for the award, it was noted that Dr. Tan "devotes his time to various marathon causes to raise funds for a wide range of charities. This includes the likes of *PolioPlus* which aims to eradicate polio, Operation Smile which provides free surgery for kids born with cleft lips, and the *Bizlink* Centre which helps the disabled in Singapore to access training and employment. Dr. Tan does all these record-breaking fundraisings despite dealing with challenges of his own such as being paralysed from the waist down due to contracting polio from age two and his leukemia diagnosis." As of mid-2018, Dr. Tan had raised over $18 million for children and medical charities.

Dr. Tan is a point of light (a person whose volunteerism shines brightly to solve the darker and more painful challenges around us). He is also a stellar example of the types of people MindChamps attracts. A 2018 study by global human resource consulting firm Robert Half showed, "35 percent of more than 1,000 workers polled said they would decline a job offer if the role was a perfect fit, but the company culture wasn't." Culture matters when it comes to attracting the talent needed to sustain it.

In 2019, to bring its Social Charter even further to the forefront, MindChamps established a registered charity called The Jameson Foundation, whose role is specifically 'to create educational opportunities and access to health-care where they would not otherwise exist.'

At MindChamps, culture starts with the actions of leadership which are reflected in the company's willingness to proudly communicate their mission, vision, values, themes, and social charter. Additionally, it involves leaders acting in accord with the words they commit to writing. It is sustained as leaders help team members focus on elements central to MindChamps' purpose.

Widening Mind and Spirit

Pandit Jawaharlal Nehru, the first Prime Minister of India, observed, "Culture is the widening of the mind and of the spirit." At MindChamps, leaders have widened their minds, spirits, and hearts. These leaders have also encouraged their team members to act in support of MindChamps' aspirational vision—"to challenge and

CHAPTER THREE

improve education standards globally". Moreover, MindChamps' leadership advances the company's vision by operationally driving behavior consistent with MindChamps' values in pursuit of the company's mission "to nurture the power of human potential for a better tomorrow."

In accord with MindChamps' social charter, leaders and frontline team members like Dr. Tan demonstrate their commitment to truly making a difference.

When it comes to culture, there is a lot that can be learned from **The MindChamps Way**.

Follow the Red Dot

- Is the vision you hold for your company, your organization, or your family shared by others or is it more like a hallucination? How do you know?
- Think about the degree to which your actions are guided by a clear sense of purpose. To what degree is your life journey similar to embarking on a long trip without knowing your destination, the purpose of your travel, or having navigational tools such as a map or GPS? What tools do you rely upon for orientation and guidance?
- Reflect on your personal or business "vision" statement. How would you rate the clarity, brevity, memorableness, and inspiration of that statement? In what ways does it reflect a dream of a better tomorrow?
- Does your personal or business mission statement offer a concise explanation of your "why" or purpose?
- Consistent with the words of Simon Sinek and the actions of MindChamps, are you leading with your "why?" More important, are you leading your life and business in the direction of your why?
- How effectively have you defined your values and the core themes? Have you communicated how acting in accord with values and themes drives your mission, which in turn makes your vision more attainable?
- How readily are you sharing your vision, mission, and values? Are you displaying them prominently inside and outside your organization? Are you talking about them and making decisions based on them?
- Consider crafting a social contract and making it public.
- What operational mechanisms have you developed to drive culture?

CHAPTER THREE

- Would the people around you be able to know your mission, vision, and values by watching your actions? If so, how?
- Give back to those you serve and encourage them to do the same.
- Let your culture widen your mind, your spirit, and your heart. Encourage a similar "widening" so team members can fully support your mission and vision!

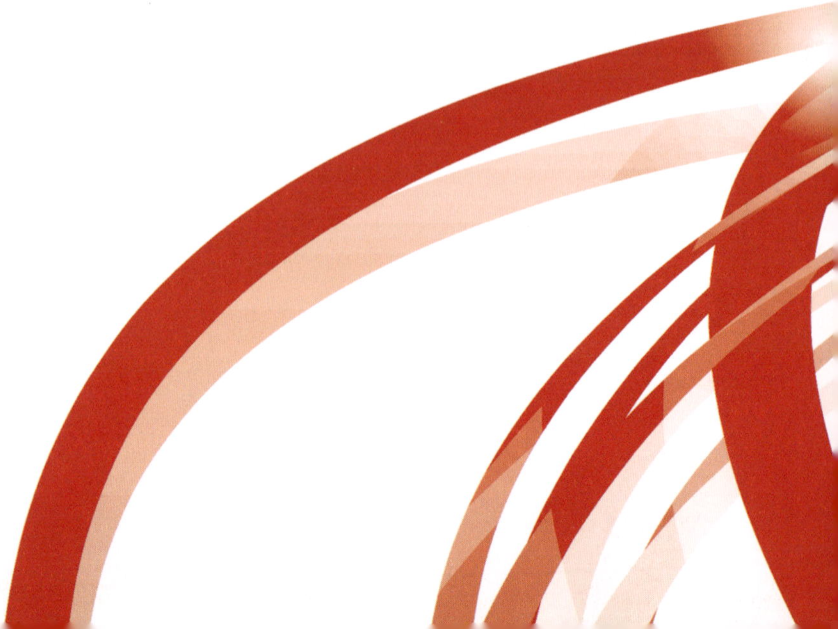

PART TWO
DELIVERING THE MOVEMENT

CHAPTER FOUR

Champion, Learning, & Creative

"The human brain, it has been said, is the most complexly organised structure in the universe... [It] is made up of one hundred billion neurons... [and] each neuron makes something like a thousand to ten thousand contacts with other neurons... [so] the number of possible permutations and combinations of brain activity, in other words the number of brain states, exceeds the number of elementary particles in the known universe.

V.S. Ramachandran
Phantoms in the Brain (B.B.C. Reith Lecture #1, 2003.)

This chapter, and the one that follows, constitute a section of the book I refer to as "**Delivering the Movement.**" In it, we will shift from MindChamps' people and culture to MindChamps' pedagogy (theory and practice of education), curriculum, and management system. This chapter will focus on the theoretical underpinnings of MindChamps' 3-Mind Model (**Champion Mind, Learning Mind and Creative Mind**).

Consistent with the work of David Chiem and Brian Caswell, we will explore the case for a fundamental revolutionary—not evolutionary—change in global education. We will also look at how MindChamps has launched a movement in support of those needed changes. Chapter five (**Driving Transformation & Growth**) closes out this section by looking at how MindChamps supports the 3-Mind Movement through its curriculum. We will also examine how MindChamps drives operational excellence to set the MindChamps ChampionGold Standard for consistency, quality, and effectiveness.

Unlike the prior segment (which focused on the business development side of MindChamps) these chapters emphasize MindChamps' educational philosophy and approach. As a business consultant, in prior chapters I offered considerable context so you could appreciate the significance of MindChamps' business accomplishments. Since educational models and educational reform are not my areas of expertise, I will honor a concept I learned from MindChamps ("know what you don't know"), and let the true experts in brain science, learning models, and educational techniques guide you. As such, expect to read a lot from MindChamps leaders David Chiem and Brian Caswell in this chapter.

One last proviso: this is only a chapter. As such, I will offer a fairly basic and cursory review of the 3-Mind model (with enough detail to help you understand the innovation and importance of the MindChamps approach). I hope this chapter will spark your learning mind and prompt you to read David Chiem and Brian Caswell's book, **The 3-Mind Revolution: A New World View for Global Leaders, Educators and Parents**. That book is thorough, accessible and enlightening. It provides metaphors, stories, and memorable examples to aid understanding of the 3-Mind approach. Thanks to the graciousness of David and Brian, this chapter will excerpt heavily from their book and weave in other ideas that surfaced during my conversations with them.

What Got Us Here Won't Get Us There

Ecclesiastes 3 in the King James Version of the Bible reads, "To every thing there is a season…a time to keep and a time to cast away." When it comes to education, David Chiem and Brian Caswell

CHAPTER FOUR

are leading a growing group of educators who believe that the seasons have changed and much needs to be tossed aside. These cutting-edge thinkers believe modern scientific findings in fields such as neuroscience should guide the creation of learning tools to meet the demands of the modern age.

Other voices advocating research-based education reform include entrepreneur, educator, and computer scientist Sebastian Thrun. Mr. Thrun noted, "If we study learning as a data science, we can reverse engineer the human brain and tailor learning techniques to maximize the chances of student success. This is the biggest revolution that could happen in education, turning it into a data-driven science, and not such a medieval set of rumors professors tend to carry on."

Writing in the foreword to David and Brian's book, Kathy Hirsh-Pasek, Leftkowitz Professor of Psychology at Temple University and senior fellow for MindChamps World Research, Advisory & Education Team, emphasizes deep change resistance in the educational system, noting, "In the mid-1980's we shifted from an industrial-based economy to a knowledge-based one. What did not change however was the education system. There is a joke that if Rip van Winkle were to awaken today, the only familiar institution in his brave new world would be the school system." These experts, and many others, agree with David Chiem and Brian Caswell's perspective concerning the antiquated state of global learning. They also support the urgent need for an educational upgrade, or in Brian and David's words, "a revolution" guided by relevant and emerging scientific breakthroughs. Since we have only scratched the surface of the problem, let's have David and Brian help us better understand the challenges ahead.

We Are Stuck in the Past

Typically, when humankind ushers in a new era of tools, lifestyle, and economic productivity, there are corresponding shifts in educational delivery. For example, when society shifted from a pre-industrial time to the Industrial Age, much changed, including:

- Movement from hand-production to factory and machine manufacturing,
- Increased use of steam power, inventive iron production,
- Job growth around manufacturing hubs,
- A redistribution of populations from rural to urban settings,
- Compulsory education for child factory workers, and
- Standardization of teaching methods, textbooks, and classroom design.

In one analysis of the U.S. educational system, titled, **The Industrial Revolution and Its Educational Impacts**, author Patrick Galvin concludes, "The impact that the Industrial revolution had on education in the United States is truly what defines education as we know it. The growth of factories and the homogenization of people to the schedule of industry spawned the 'factory model' for schools to follow. Teachers' roles were taken seriously enough to create training schools specifically for their skills. Education in general moved away from a right of privilege to a societal necessity. A growing democracy was mimicked closely by a changing educational system."

The Industrial Revolution and the "factory model" of education it produced has had significant benefits and drawbacks. From the perspective of educational advantages, the Industrial Revolution brought standardization of teaching methods and greater educational access beyond the children of the elite.

CHAPTER FOUR

Books were more easily manufactured and consistent methods of evaluation were developed to assess a student's ability to memorize, read, spell, or do math problems.

David and Brian provide a thoughtful analysis of the nuances and complexities of educational changes in the industrial age:

"…universal mass education was a 19th Century innovation. It did not, however, come about through some altruistic belief that it should be the right of every child to have an education—though forward thinking reformers believed that way. Universal education grew out of the need to have workers with at least enough education to function—in the factories and the offices…This was why 19th and early 20th Century mass education concentrated on the '3R's'—Reading, 'Riting and 'Rithmetic. A broader education was still the domain of the privileged class. Curriculum content was limited to what was deemed necessary to know. The content was set, and delivered, by authority figures. Learning consisted of passively memorising given information with the aim of regurgitating it at a later date, and a minimum of critical analysis of what was being taught…Although the scope of school curricula gradually broadened, the essential approach remained the same… And it worked, for a period of time."

In the 1939 movie The Wizard of Oz, lead character Dorothy Gale is rendered unconscious by flying debris from a tornado that hits near her family's farm in the US state of Kansas. As she awakes in Munchkinland in the Land of Oz, she is accompanied by her dog Toto. Realizing she is in very unfamiliar surroundings, Dorothy says,

"Toto, I've a feeling we're not in Kansas anymore." As a society, we aren't in the "industrial age anymore," but according to David Chiem and Brian Caswell, the current educational system behaves as if we are.

Welcome to the Information and Technology Age

In ***The 3-Mind Revolution***, David and Brian advocate for dramatic educational reform to bring education in alignment with two major trends, "Today, we are in the midst of a significant global transition. New technologies have opened up a universe of information with infinite possibilities, but, sadly we are still approaching this amazing resource with the old school mindset of passive learning."

Let's look at the social impact of the two forces David and Brian identified above—information and technology. Most social commentators suggest the Information Age began in the 1970s and continues strong today. It has been called by other names such as the digital age, the computer age, and the new media age, but it is marked by increased production, transmission, and use of information. While the Internet was developed in the 1970s, back then it was little more than a communication platform for scientists and government entities. A proliferation of personal computers, the development of fiber optic cables, and faster microprocessors all summated in the commercialization of what we now know to be the World Wide Web. In short order, many of us experienced the birth of electronic mail (better known as email) and the so-called democratization of information.

Andrew Sonstrom, technical writer for *Deep Core Data*, shares how the information revolution has fueled a corresponding technological revolution, noting, "The Industrial Age began somewhere around 300 years ago, and lasted right up until about 30 years ago when the internet was in its infancy. While there was a notable acceleration of progress from that of the Agricultural Age, it still took lifetimes before real change in technology took hold. In the early stages of the Information Age, it took decades, and now, technological advancement has accelerated even further, to the point where new technology is released multiple times a year."

As was the case with the transition into the Industrial Age, an explosion of information and technology have created learning opportunities as well as sizable challenges. From a pure mental processing or learning perspective, technology appears to be shortening attention spans. In a 2017 article for the National Alliance on Mental Illness (NAMI), psychologist Jyothsna Bhat, PsyD suggests that adults are overwhelmed by constant inbound neural inputs and that, "Our children are experiencing the same stimulation, while developmentally they're also learning how to organize information and pay attention. Bombarded with excessive stimulation…they are expected to focus on subjects that may not hold their interest the same way other stimulating, instantly gratifying subjects do. The brain is trained at a young age to multitask to such a high degree that it is often incapable of focusing on one task or thought at a time."

The information age is also having discernible impact in the context of business. Julian Birkinshaw, Professor and Chair of Strategy and Entrepreneurship at the London Business School, wrote an article for **Wired** magazine in which he reviewed corporate information processing challenges. According to Professor Birkinshaw, individuals in business life often "face two contrasting risks. One is that we become obsessed with getting to the bottom of a problem, and we keep on digging, desperate to find the truth but taking forever to do so. The other risk is that we become overwhelmed with the amount of information out there and we give up: we realise we cannot actually master the issue at hand, and we end up falling back on a pre-existing belief." These risks may be the byproduct of passive learning strategies experienced by those who currently live in the workforce.

David Chiem and Brian Caswell warn that residual passive learning strategies developed for the Industrial Age fail to help children learn in what they call a "post-Pentium" world. Moreover, they suggest we should be using scientific knowledge to advance beyond passive learning:

> "In order to understand the limitations of traditional passive learning strategies, it is important to understand the incredible strengths and the very real limitations of our remarkable human brain. Many of our insights into the nature of the learning brain are recent–the result of breakthroughs during the last 20 or 30 years in the fields of neuroscience, psychology, information technology…."

Let's recap for a moment. We have an education system that was optimized for the Industrial Age attempting to prepare children for a world inundated with information and marked by attention-robbing technologies. At the same time, we have burgeoning fields of science that can help guide the development of learning tools which will enable success in current and future times. It is in this context that David and Brian call for urgent action:

CHAPTER FOUR

"…we use the word revolution very deliberately–because unlike evolution which implies a passive and gradual response, revolution implies action and positive intent.

Because, in a world created by the exponential growth of digital technology, it is quite simply, too late for a gradual evolution…

We are creative adaptive, intelligent creatures with the innate capacity to respond to change and meet it with innovation …we must accept that a new world demands a new way of thinking. And that a new way of thinking demands a better way of preparing the mind."

This is MindChamps' foundation for *The 3-Mind Revolution*!

Exploring the 3-Mind Model and the Champion Mind

In chapter two, as we explored important leadership mindsets possessed by David Chiem, I alluded to the 3 Minds: champion, learning, and creative. For the purpose of understanding the MindChamps learning model, let's explore each of these 3 Minds and look at the importance of providing tools to develop them. Along the way, Brian and David can help us begin to appreciate the scientific understandings that support the MindChamps Model.

In *The 3-Mind Revolution*, David and Brian suggest that "in this brave new world, the ability to cope with change will mark the difference between success and failure. This means developing three distinct minds: i) The Champion Mind, ii) The Learning Mind, and iii) The Creative Mind."

As you will recall from chapter two, the term Champion Mind is credited to MindChamps Chair of Research, Professor

Allan Snyder. His scientific study and observation gave life to the Champion Mind construct which can be roughly defined as a thinking framework that mentally prepares a person for success. According to David and Brian, the Champion Mind blends together equal amounts of emotional intelligence, communication skills, self-awareness, and self-confidence. They noted that Professor Snyder's "breakthrough discovery is that the Champion Mindset is not some mysterious quality only present in a few lucky individuals. His research clearly demonstrates that the elements of a Champion Mindset can actually be learned." As mentioned earlier, Professor Snyder studied champions worldwide through events such as the spectacularly successful 'What Makes a Champion?' forum in conjunction with the Sydney 2000 and the Beijing 2008 Olympic Games and the 'What Makes a Young Champion' at the Singapore 2010 Youth Olympic Games.

Through these studies, he demonstrated a truth that is both simple and profound.

David and Brian summarize Professor Snyder's research on the Champion Mind in the following way:

> "Champions abhor being ordinary. They make a conscious decision to identify themselves and broadcast it. In this way, they leave their individual mark on everything they do. Champions are willing to transcend conventional wisdom. If the old way doesn't work they quickly find a new way. Champions also develop the ability to accept and learn from adversity."

As to the last point, Professor Allan Snyder expounds on the role of adversity in the context of the Champion Mind in his book ***What Makes a Champion!***. According to Professor Snyder, "Champions are often familiar with adversity…They learn how to convert, as McKinsey's Michael Rennie says, 'upsets into set-ups' for something better… Many of the world's greatest scientists were at best average students… Struggling in the early learning process possibly acclimatizes us to difficulties, and may advantage us in dealing with adversity because we then see difficulties as being a matter of course."

According to David Chiem and Brian Caswell, there are a litany of successful people who could be characterized in Professor Snyder's words as being "at best, average students." Many of them had teachers who expressly doubted their future potential. Undaunted, their Champion Mind prevailed and we know them as Steve Jobs, Sir Richard Branson, Steven Spielberg, and even Albert Einstein. In addition to their perseverance, these individuals also shared a love for learning.

Exploring the Learning Mind

MindChamps leaders have extensively studied brain function and factors that facilitate learning skill development and knowledge acquisition. In their book, ***The 3-Mind Revolution***, David and Brian highlight a number of important research breakthroughs emerging from paleophysiology (the science of the physiological evolution of animals) and neuroscience. Those breakthroughs include an understanding of how the mammalian brain (and more specifically the human brain) benefits from neuronal pathways that link learning to memory. In The **3-Mind Revolution**, David and Brian note, "Mammals…are capable of changing their behavior within their own life-times as a result of experience, rather than waiting for a genetic mutation to fortuitously kick-start the change in some future generation. This is something pretty unique in the animal kingdom, and it is a result of the fact that unlike reptiles, fish, amphibians, insects and (probably) dinosaurs — mammals have emotions…

You see, emotions are, essentially the key to all learning. All incoming sensory data is processed by the limbic system — which is the seat of emotion, as well as acting as an information clearing house and the first stage in the process of creating memories."

The unique and important role of emotions in the learning process can be found in a large body of research, such as a 2017 article for the journal Frontiers in Psychology titled the "Influences of Emotion and Learning." In that article, researchers Chai M. Tyng, Hafeez U. Amin, Mohamad N. M. Saad, and Aamir S. Malik report that many studies have shown varied thinking (cognitive) process, "are affected by emotions, including attention…learning and memory…reasoning…and problem-solving…These factors are critical in educational domains because when students face such difficulties, it defeats the purpose of schooling and can potentially render it meaningless. Most importantly, emotional stimuli appear to consume more attentional resources than non-emotional stimuli…Moreover, attentional and motivational components of emotion have been linked to heightened learning and memory… Hence, emotional experiences/stimuli appear to be remembered vividly and accurately, with great resilience over time."

For leaders at MindChamps, understanding the powerful interconnection between emotions and learning shapes the

CHAPTER FOUR

educational environment created at MindChamps centers. Specifically, David and Brian note, "How we feel when we learn something strongly influences our future experience of the learning. Things learned under a cloud of fear, anxiety, shame, anger, or frustration will generate echoes of those emotions every time the learning is accessed, and as we are naturally repelled by such feelings, we become reluctant to revisit the learning."

In addition to crafting an emotionally positive learning environment and strategically building emotional learning strategies into MindChamps' curriculum, leaders are helping learners develop skills to manage information overload in the modern age. The term "information overload" is credited to Betram Gross, a political science professor at Hunter College. It can be traced back to 1964 and Gross' two-part publication titled, *The Managing of Organizations*. Information overload gained widespread use approximately six years later with the release of Alvin Toffler's book titled "**Future Shock**," in which Toffler suggests a state of overload occurs "if overstimulation at the sensory level increases the distortion with which we perceive reality."

From his vantage point in 1970, Toffler suggested that, "By instructing students how to learn, unlearn and relearn, a powerful new dimension can be added to education." Toffler goes on to cite psychologist Herbert Gerjouy who predicted that in the future educators will need to "teach the individual how to classify and reclassify information, how to evaluate its veracity, how to change categories when necessary, how to move from the concrete to the abstract and back, how to look at problems from a new direction— how to teach himself. Tomorrow's illiterate will not be the man who can't read; he will be the man who has not learned how to learn."

Welcome to the future, as forecast by Alvin Toffler! MindChamps is responding to the realities of Toffler's accurate future prediction. As such, MindChamps' curriculum teaches children how to classify information, evaluate its veracity, and essentially "learn how to learn" in the age of information overload. Brian and David note:

> "The model we have developed to describe the skills and techniques required to train the Learning Mind effectively, is based on decades of working with learners at all levels and ages.
>
> We call it the Hourglass Model and it differs from more traditional models because it stresses:
>
> i) Managing information on a 'need to know, want to know' basis;
>
> ii) Active understanding, storage and recall of relevant information and concepts; and
>
> iii) Synthesis and expression strategies, to create and communicate new understandings and innovations.
>
> The exciting thing about the Hourglass Model is that it works in both innovative situations and more traditional learning environments. This is because the focus is on training and effective learning habits, rather than drilling content."

The last element in the Hourglass model involves helping learners to synthesize and express concepts such that those concepts can be used to fuel creativity and innovation. In keeping with the importance of innovation in the digital age, MindChamps' leaders have invested considerably to understand ways to fuel the creative mind.

Exploring the Creative Mind

In **The 3-Mind Revolution**, David and Brian begin their discussion of creativity in the context of research on brain lateralization, noting, "Although the distinctions between 'right-brain' and 'left brain' functions have been drastically overstated for decades, there is enough evidence of left/right lateral differentiation to allow us to still speak, in metaphorical terms of the 'creative right brain' and the 'structured and logical left brain.'"

A 2017 **Frontiers of Psychology** article written by University of Auckland Professor Michael Corballis confirms David and Brian's perspective concerning the complex yet established research on lateralization. Professor Corballis observes, "It has become clear that cerebral asymmetries are more complex and multidimensional, both in terms of their circuitry and their genetic underpinnings. Moreover, cerebral asymmetries are never absolute; even in a strongly left-lateralized function…"

According to David and Brian, research conducted by Professor Allan Snyder, has been particularly important when it comes to lateralization and creativity:

> "In a recent experiment (dubbed the 'Thinking Cap' experiment and featured in media outlets across the world), Professor Snyder demonstrated how the ability to solve a novel problem was significantly increased, if activity in the left fronto-temporal lobe was reduced, using Transcranial

Direct-Current Stimulation (tDCS). In the press, this was referred to as 'switching on creativity'...

What it clearly demonstrated, was that the dominance of 'left-brain' processes can negatively affect our ability to think 'outside the box' – that when we become habituated to certain ways of doing things, it can be almost impossible to do things a different way even if the old way isn't working well.

Reduce that dominance, even temporarily, and our natural propensity for finding new and different solutions re-asserts itself."

These findings have rather important implications for the creation of learning environments and learning tasks. Specifically, Professors Chunfang Zhou and Aparna Purushothaman from Aalborg University in Denmark writing in the *International Journal of Emerging Technologies in Learning* (IJET) suggest educators should create school environments that produce what Zhou and Purushothaman call "cultures of creativity." In their article, these Professors indicate the importance of developing an educational setting that abandons "the passivity of learning, and seeks opportunities for creativity, social connections, and personal growth. It means...beginning to reject the 'sit back and be told' school culture...." In what Professors Zhou and Purushothaman have shown to be a more optimized way to address creative skills for the digital age, these researchers encourage teachers to give students opportunities to collaborate and "ask questions, explore different strategies of investigation, and create their own solutions... Rather than displaying laminated examples of the 'best answer' on the walls, these classrooms show work in progress, experiments, even things that have gone wrong. They encourage a 'hands-on' approach to learning, and a spirit of enquiry and questioning."

MindChamps leaders have translated their knowledge of the science of brain function and creativity to help children "avoid anti-creative learning practices like rote-learning and drilling." Alternatively, they have developed learning tools which help children develop crafted imagination which results in effectively achieving a creative purpose.

Unifying the Power of the 3-Mind Approach

The MindChamps approach addresses ways to foster the flawless integration of the Champion Mind, the Learning Mind, and the Creative Mind. It challenges passive learning and "factory-like" curriculum which are vestiges from the Industrial Age. MindChamps' multi-disciplinary science-based approach has led to curriculum development suited to guide students to learn how to learn (more on that curriculum in chapter five). I'll close this chapter with the clear objectives designed into MindChamps' 3-Mind approach, as stated by David and Brian:

> "If we can train the Champion Mind to develop its unique strengths and to recognize the strengths of others, we have a solid foundation upon which to build other skills.
> If we can develop the Learning Mind, so that we maintain our natural curiosity about the world, and construct, store and use knowledge effectively, we will be able to break through our obsession with detail and focus on how we learn.

If we can develop, in the Creative Mind, the imagination and the discipline to apply creativity to the problems we face, and if we strive, in our education systems, to give creativity the strong emphasis that it deserves, we can build a world in which everyone has the opportunity and the capability to contribute."

Based on the results you will read in chapter six, I suspect you will conclude that these objectives are not aspirations or ifs. They are real outcomes occurring now at MindChamps. They are a movement that characterizes **The MindChamps Way**.

CHAPTER FOUR

(Rather than asking you to reflect on the content from this Chapter, this "Follow the Red Dot" section highlights the rich content David and Brian shared throughout this chapter.)

Follow the Red Dot

- Educational delivery changed to meet the needs of an industrial society but has failed to keep pace with the demands of the information and technology age.
- Among the most troublesome and outdated elements of education today are passive learning, an emphasis on memorization, and a prioritization of content over skill development.
- Given the pace of information dissemination, new technologies are emerging at an unprecedented rate.
- The digital age has resulted in constant mental activation and is affecting attention spans and the way we process information.
- Given the gap between 21st Century educational needs and the existing educational system, David Chiem and Brian Caswell suggest an urgent revolution (as opposed to a more prolonged evolution).
- The 3-Mind Revolution involves the development of three distinct minds: i) The Champion Mind, ii) The Learning Mind, and iii) The Creative Mind.
- As per Professor Allan Snyder, the Champion Mind is demonstrated by an individual who abhors being ordinary.
- Champions are willing to transcend conventional wisdom.
- Champions develop the ability to accept and learn from adversity.
- The Champion Mind is equal parts emotional intelligence, communication skills, self-awareness, and self-confidence.
- Emotions are essentially the key to all learning.

- The powerful interconnection between emotion and learning must be considered in creating the right educational environment for young learners.
- As per predictions of Alvin Toffler in 1970 (echoing the words of Herbert Jouroy), "Tomorrow's illiterate will not be the man who can't read; he will be the man who has not learned how to learn."
- The MindChamps' Hourglass model helps learners acquire, sort, retain, and synthesize information for use in creative and expressive ways.
- Based on research conducted by Professor Snyder, David Chiem and Brian Caswell conclude, "The dominance of 'left-brain' processes can negatively affect our ability to think 'outside the box'."
- To help develop children who will create needed future innovation, educators should "avoid anti-creative learning practices like rote-learning and drilling." Alternatively, they must help children develop "crafted imagination" which results in effectively achieving "creative purpose."

CHAPTER FIVE

Driving Transformation and Growth

"All your ideas may be solid or even good...But you have to Actually EXECUTE on them for them to matter."

Gary Vaynerchuck
Social Media Entrepreneur, Author, and Speaker

The keywords in this chapter title are transformation and growth. They are chosen to emphasize how leaders at MindChamps facilitate multiple levels of change within and across the organization. For example, the beginning of this chapter will explore how MindChamps uses its 3-Mind Model to develop effective curriculum and optimal learning environments. Later in this chapter, we will examine how MindChamps drives operational consistency on a global basis.

As you will soon see, leaders at MindChamps take a structured yet progressive approach to product and process excellence. In turn, their well-organized efforts result in heightened productivity, enhanced innovation, and sustainable business growth. Much of MindChamps' transformative leadership is reflected in operational discipline that has produced an efficient management system to support MindChamps centers around the world.

The link between leadership discipline and organizational

excellence is well summarized in an ***Industry Week*** article by Brian Rains (a chemical engineer who led Dupont's Global Operations Excellence Practice). In that article, titled "**The Path to Operational Excellence Through Operational Discipline**," Brian notes, "Leadership is essential to establishing the appropriate organizational structure and focused processes that will improve operational excellence. Leadership articulates and defines the shared values and common purpose and prioritizes the things that truly matter to drive the highest levels of operational excellence. The direction needed to support this is delivered to the organization through proper tools and training, as well as employee involvement, clear communication of the rules, open dialogue and alignment." In chapter three, we discussed MindChamps' shared values and common purpose. This chapter looks at how MindChamps' leaders craft tools, training, and open dialogue to create consistency, transformation, and growth for teachers, parents, children, communities, the global education system, and the MindChamps brand.

From Theory to Application

In a conversation with Brian Caswell, MindChamps' Dean of Research and Development, it became clear that MindChamps activates the 3-Mind model through a mix of art and science. Brian shares, "The model guides us to help children develop their Champion mind, Learning mind, and Creative mind. It also frames the skills we seek to enhance so children can succeed in the 21st century." Brian adds, "We begin with our desired outcomes. We then merge educational best practices with our experience as educators. Through that process, we explore new and exciting

CHAPTER FIVE

ways to design learning, guide teacher training, and structure our PreSchools to achieve transformative success." Brian suggests that MindChamps curriculum designers identify the skill development needs of learners, delineate a clear list of learning goals, create a curriculum matrix to guide the sequencing of learning components, specify instructional methods (e.g., group, hands-on, and independent exploration), and establish ongoing mechanisms for evaluating learning effectiveness.

He notes that MindChamps is in a continual process of "testing various curriculum elements. We have been doing this for two decades and we will never stop seeking to be a little better tomorrow than we are today. We also expect our teachers to stay within the framework of our curriculum, while infusing it with passion and creativity to make each lesson learner-centric. This means every teacher personalizes their experience delivery to the unique needs and goals of each student. In so doing, they partner with each child and with their parents to deliver learning that involves, motivates, and maximizes potential."

MindChamps' CEO David Chiem focuses on how formal research is integrated into curriculum development by noting, "Our MindChamps World Research, Advisory & Education Team is continually researching. Their findings are being used to inform and guide MindChamps' curriculum design. We do case studies on our successful initiatives and transfer insights into the daily lives of our centers through tangible tools and ongoing teacher training. Curriculum design and the delivery of that curriculum through our learning environment is a never ending, invigorating, and fundamental component for discovery and growth at MindChamps and for the discovery and growth of our teachers and students."

Writing in **The Smart Local Singapore**, commentator Cheryl Lee describes and offers insights on MindChamps' well-crafted curriculum. Ms. Lee's perspective was shared after she shadowed a MindChamps PreSchool teacher, Ms. Deanna, for a day. In her article, Ms. Lee suggests the experience gave her "insight into the depth of the research and thinking that goes behind their unique curriculum that distinguishes MindChamps PreSchool from the rest." Specifically, Ms. Lee notes how MindChamps students (referred to as Champs) begin their day with teachers supervising "temperature-taking and sanitizing of hands and feet." She describes how English skill development was enhanced through a creative approach, noting Ms. Deanna took "the class on a make-believe adventure" where students prepared a "pretend 'alphabet soup'."

Ms. Lee goes on to describe Chinese Class, free expression time, enrichment in the MindChamps NeuroMooves™ gym, breaks, snacks, lunch, nap time, and departure. In describing activities, she suggests, "Champs explore their creativity", experience "plenty of running, laughter, and fun," and enhance "brain development, coordination and balance." Ms. Lee concludes that all of this was done while Ms. Deanna spoke "nicely but firmly to inculcate the MindChamps Education and Life Philosophy of '100% Respect and Zero Fear'."

MindChamps' curriculum is clearly designed to enhance champion, learning, and creative abilities. It is created methodically, and it constantly evolves. Let's take a moment to look at how the MindChamps curriculum comes to life as part of the broader MindChamps learning environment.

CHAPTER FIVE

The Learning Environment – A Joinder of Physical Elements and Human Care

When it comes to the MindChamps PreSchool, four elements drive the brand's quality:
- Curriculum,
- Environment,
- Teachers, and
- Leaders.

Since we just highlighted curriculum development and will be reviewing leadership and teacher excellence toward the end of the chapter (in the context of MindChamps management system), let's take a moment to understand some of the important elements of the MindChamps PreSchool environment.

Everyone who works at a MindChamps PreSchool is responsible for the quality of the learning milieu. Additionally, MindChamps has a quality assurance team that monitors each establishment to guarantee they conform with MindChamps' standards as well as governmental regulatory requirements.

MindChamps designs each center to be an intentional learning environment with "specific outcomes or goals in mind that support the curriculum, theme, and young children's overall development." MindChamps views this intentional learning setting to be a function of the physical layout of the center and human factors created by administrators, teachers, and other center team members. Intentional teachers, for example, are tasked with providing clearly defined learning objectives and employing purposeful strategies that help children achieve those objectives. Intentional teachers also assess the progress of the individual child, and adjust strategies based on observations.

MindChamps provides precise guidelines for the layout, maintenance, and use of all areas in the center. We will briefly touch on the reception area and the learning environment.

The entry or reception area of a MindChamps PreSchool serves many important functions, not the least of which is the creation of a visually inviting initial experience for all who enter. It is also a place to display the purposeful creativity of MindChamps learners and it provides parents a notice board to foster communication. The reception area offers secure access and egress via its identity tracking system and it houses a health check station, a shoe rack, all government operating licenses and other relevant regulatory disclosures.

Typically, when individuals outside of education think of learning environments, they conjure up images of classrooms, chalkboards, and desks.

The MindChamps PreSchool classroom is different. It includes a 'Connecting-as-One' area and six 'Learning Zones'. The Connecting-as-One area is the place where an entire class can circle around to engage greetings, offer show and tell, experience stories, play games, and receive instructions on activities that will occur in the learning zones.

The six learning zones in a MindChamps PreSchool are based on inquiry learning — where children follow, individually or in groups, areas of interest, based on questions drawn from their own experiences and the teacher's input. The zones are further divided into two lobes:

Imagination
- Dramatic
- Arts & Crafts

- Construction

Skills
- Numeracy
- Reading
- Writing

Since the learning focus of each zone can be inferred from its name, I will simply illustrate the types of resources available for Inquiry Learning.

In an article for the New York City Department of Education written by teachers Melissa Fine and Lindsey Desmond, the Inquiry Learning approach is described as one where "children pose meaningful questions and are encouraged to solve problems by experimenting and evaluating possible solutions. Teachers guide children to apply this newly constructed knowledge to broaden, analyze, critique, and ultimately defend new hypotheses. The teacher's role within this framework is that of a facilitator, guiding learners to explore their questions and decide on a course of action. Teachers pose carefully crafted, open-ended questions that allow learners to deepen their thinking and investigate further, rather than respond with one correct or incorrect answer."

As such, the MindChamps' Inquiry Learning Zones are equipped with:
- Natural objects (e.g., shells and leaves),
- Living things (e.g., insects and plants),
- Scientific resources (e.g., magnets and magnifying glasses),
- Exploratory resources (e.g., phones and models of body parts),
- Practical experimental activities, and

- Posters, books, and games related to children's/teacher's inquiry question(s) and themes.

The Construction Zone supports what is referred to by educators as "construction play" or "constructing play." At MindChamps, it involves children manipulating items in the zone. Through this process, children develop fine and gross motor skills. They enhance problem-solving and adaptive thinking skills. Children also learn to plan, persevere, and work effectively with others.

The MindChamps Construction Zone is sourced with:
- Large blocks and construction sets,
- Small manipulative sets,
- Dramatic props, and
- Visual resources.

According to leaders at MindChamps, it is critical to provide an enriched and well-designed physical environment. Additionally, that environment must be supported by well-trained teachers to, in David Chiem's words, "release, focus, and turn" each child's potential into success. In the learning zones, for example, MindChamps requires teachers to:

- "Plan appropriate learning activities to enhance and enrich the Champs' knowledge, skills and learning experiences.
- Provide ample opportunities for the Champs to work alone and in small groups.
- Be mindful to provide opportunities to cater to the different learning styles of the Champs.
- Provide opportunities for the Champs to explore, problem-solve and predict solutions independently or as a group.
- Encourage the Champs to ask investigative questions and conduct their own investigations."

CHAPTER FIVE

As Brian Caswell puts it, "MindChamps teachers are trained to 'Observe, Reflect and Respond' to everything that occurs in the room, with the child's engagement as the primary directive."

David uses a metaphor from his background as an actor to describe the orchestrated interplay of factors needed to create the optimal MindChamps experience, saying, "You can liken what we do to simultaneously producing and delivering global theatrical performances. Imagine you have an extraordinary script, perfectly designed stages, consummate stage crews and production teams, and you have selected the best acting talent possible. Now, imagine you want your theater production to be presented flawlessly to every audience, every night. That is our challenge each day around the world. In our case, however, the outcome of our performance has far greater impact than pleasing an audience through entertainment. We must deliver transformative skills every day, every time, for every child and for generations to come."

David goes on to note, "There is a gap within the gap, which can affect the quality of experience a child enjoys. Even if a school has its own philosophy and unique pedagogy, all too often, teachers are thrown into their role without training in the specifics of that methodology. This is like taking a cast of professional actors, even Oscar winners, and asking them to go before a live audience without rehearsal. For that reason, we require all of our teachers to be immersed in the MindChamps way of nurturing the 3 Minds. They receive up to 200 hours of training and accreditation through our PreSchool Teachers' training institute, the MindChamps Mindset Academy."

This Academy is another element unique to the MindChamps model. It's core training team is tasked with the provision of training 'above and beyond' formal teaching qualifications and regulatory requirements, and this training is compulsory for all teachers — regardless of their previous experience.

As Brian Caswell explains, "We want our teachers to have cutting-edge skills and alignment with our model and our values. We want them to offer quality learning experiences from the heart. But, most of all, we want them to realize that 'better' doesn't mean 'more difficult' — that teaching effectively, that is, in a child-centred, inquiry-oriented way, is generally more fun, and far less stressful, than using out-dated, ineffectual methods"

The proof of this philosophy is seen in the fact that the training is extremely popular with MindChamps teachers.

Ms. Heather Duncan, a British teacher working for MindChamps in the UAE says "The training has really opened my eyes to different ways of thinking about teaching, and especially effective leadership."

Ellie Sykes, a MindChamps teacher trained in Australia, shares: "I am so happy to be part of the MindChamps Family! The focus on role-play gets you out of your comfort zone and allows you to explore new ideas and challenges. I feel much more confident and knowledgeable," and another Australian teacher, Clare Woodham, added, "The training was interesting, fun and interactive. I have gained valuable knowledge, which I can use in the classroom… This training programme is fantastic!'

Esteemed psychologist Carl Jung addressed the importance of blending teacher skills, human warmth, and a solid curriculum, noting, "One looks back with appreciation to the brilliant teachers, but with gratitude to those who touched our human feelings. The curriculum is so much necessary raw material, but warmth is the

CHAPTER FIVE

vital element for the growing plant and for the soul of the child."

Since we've highlighted teacher onboarding and training, let's examine how MindChamps drives consistent excellence into every student interaction. We will do this by focusing on the MindChamps franchise model and management system. We will also explore MindChamps' commitment to ongoing development of the leadership and teacher talent needed to deliver a consistent and optimal MindChamps Experience.

Every Child, Every Time, Everywhere

Over the course of my career, I have had the opportunity to consult for a number of brands that rely on other business entities to distribute their products and services. In some cases (like Starbucks' partnership with the Alibaba group in China), these distribution models involve joint ventures in which each party is responsible for managing operations. In other cases, such as International Dairy Queen's U.S. operation, the arrangement reflects a licensing or franchise model—wherein Dairy Queen licenses marketing, business processes, and Dairy Queen's products and services to independent restauranteurs.

When handled well, franchisee/licensing models create a win/win/win. The franchisor grows through the reach of its franchise community, the franchisee leverages the franchisor's core competencies, and consumers benefit from access and predictable product delivery.

In her MBA thesis at the University of Pretoria, Letlhogonolo Thobejane describes franchisors and franchisees shared role, noting, "For the franchise model—which essentially involves a team working collectively to achieve common goals—to be successful, product and service quality should be consistent with what the brand promises. The ultimate responsibility in delivering this promise rests with franchisees, and therefore, their commitment is paramount to the sustainability and effective management of the franchise brand." Since franchisees ultimately deliver student experiences in the markets they serve, MindChamps exercises extreme discretion when selecting franchisees.

David notes, "Our franchise model grew rapidly because more than 70% of our franchisees were parents of our students, who had first-hand experience of the MindChamps way. Many of these people were corporate executives, who discovered a new calling — that they wanted to make a difference. By partnering with MindChamps, through the franchise model, they were able to fulfil that calling and expand the reach of the MindChamps approach."

Ms. Lynn Chew and Ms. Gail Lim , co-franchisees of two MindChamps centers tell a typical story. Lynn shares, "I sent my child to MindChamps three years ago because I was so impressed with the learning environment and curriculum. And because I totally believed with the brand, I was convinced to take up a MindChamps PreSchool Franchise together with my friend." Gail agrees that her experience as a MindChamps parent was instrumental in her becoming a franchisee. She adds, "The past three years have been very fruitful and rewarding journey because we were able to fulfil our priorities as mothers without sacrificing our career. It's great to be working with an established brand like MindChamps PreSchool."

But individual franchisees are only part of the story. MindChamps international expansion is fueled by partnerships with

CHAPTER FIVE

a series of international 'master franchisees'. It is a unique — and particularly effective aspect of the MindChamps model.

As David explains, "One of the advantages we've experienced is that our partners seek us out after they have searched for the global benchmark in early childhood education. As such, they approach us to bring MindChamps educational solutions to their nations. We are careful only to appoint partners whom we assess as capable and willing to adopt and run our centers as we've designed them, but that means nothing unless their values are aligned with ours."

David describes his franchisee partners as "special business leaders and active entrepreneurs who invest considerable time and effort to train team members and operate their centers to provide MindChamps transformational experiences. Since we require all MindChamps teachers to be trained and accredited directly by the core training team from our MindChamps Teachers' Academy and given the significant amount of time that this training involves, if a prospective franchisee is unwilling to do what is required, there can be no partnership. We are blessed with partners, internationally, who fully embrace what it takes to operate from excellence."

The remainder of this chapter explores key elements of the MindChamps management system referred to as the ChampionGold Standard. This proprietary operating system outlines exacting performance criteria in three overarching domains:

- Teaching and learning,
- Leadership, and
- Culture and relationship (a preview of which was provided in chapter three).

To achieve success in each of these areas, MindChamps guides leaders and team members in all centers (company owned and franchise) by providing:
- Clearly defined standards,
- Established policies and protocols,
- Compulsory training of leaders and frontline team members,
- Ongoing support and consultation to achieve continuous improvement, and
- Rigorous performance monitoring.

While I will be using the leadership domain to illustrate the types of guidance and structure provided by MindChamps, please realize similar resources are provided to support the culture and relationship and teaching and learning domains.

MindChamps ChampionGold Standard — 100% Respect, Zero Fear

The art of greatness does not involve inventing everything from scratch. Often it requires seeing what others are doing effectively and adapting those elements to your situation. In my book The New Gold Standard, I explain how leaders at The Ritz-Carlton Hotel company routinely seek inspiration and best practices from other businesses, noting, "Over the years, the leadership team at Ritz-Carlton 'closed gaps' in their business processes by imitating and innovating from the best practices of other trend-setting organizations. For example, realizing that Ritz-Carlton lacked a well-defined process for designing new products and services, leadership directly implemented the Xerox Corporation's six step approach to quality improvement…Federal Express was studied

CHAPTER FIVE

to look for systematic ways to deliver products and services at Ritz-Carlton."

Similarly, MindChamps looked to the service basics of the Ritz-Carlton when establishing fundamental elements leaders should aspire to create at every MindChamps center. This is reflected in a commitment to provide "a warm welcome, great learning, and a fond farewell."

David shared a story that encapsulates his approach to learning from the best:

"One of Newton's most famous lines," he said, "is 'if I have seen further, it is by standing on the shoulders of giants.' Most people know this quote, and it makes perfect sense. We all draw on the wisdom of those who went before us. I prefer, however, to look at the example of Einstein, who is famous for his ability to 'think outside the square'. In order to explain the universe anew, he first had to master and understand Newtonian physics, but in order to innovate — to create a new science for a new century — he had to move beyond the old models and challenge convention. This shows a philosophy of '100% Respect, Zero Fear' — a concept coined by MindChamps, and the philosophy that drives the entire organisation."

Being MindChamps, therefore, leveraging on the success of others is balanced, inevitably, with the key tenets of the Champion Mindset — particularly the notion of an abhorrence to being 'just ordinary'; of expressing your unique vision — and David Chiem's unique vision for excellence focused on the prime importance of leadership.

As he has stated, "There is no teamwork without leadership. There is no growth without leadership. There are no standards without leadership. Therefore, our primary imperative must be to develop the leadership potential of every team-member."

The MindChamps ChampionGold Standard literature specifically asserts that 'the quality of leadership within our schools will influence the quality of all aspects of school life,' and so important was this assertion, in fact, that in 2008, MindChamps established the MindChamps Leadership Academy, with the specific goal of nurturing leadership potential throughout the organization.

The MindChamps ChampionGold Standard develops, sustains, and enhances leaders in the context of leadership precepts, professional values, and target areas (referred to at MindChamps as protocols), and those precepts, values and protocols form the basis of the training provided in the Leadership Academy.

In essence, this emphasis on developing the quality of leadership at every level of the organization is one of the key elements that makes MindChamps different from other companies I have studied.

In order to understand the effectiveness of the MindChamps leadership model, it is best to take a moment to reflect on the underlying principles upon which that model is founded. Here, we have the advantage that David Chiem has clearly articulated the underlying precepts of what he refers to as 'Trinity Leadership'.

It is a concept that he explains succinctly, yet effectively, in his up-coming book, **Trinity Leadership**, and I highly recommend that you take the time to read, in depth, about the essence and the genesis of the three key precepts that underpin the Trinity Leadership model.

For now, I will summarise the three precepts, and then we will examine how they influence the quality of leadership throughout the

CHAPTER FIVE

MindChamps organization — and how that quality is evaluated and maintained through the application of the ChampionGold Standard.

The Three Precepts of the leadership trinity focus on Self, Thinking and Strategy and can be represented in the above diagram:

- **Self**—Leaders are encouraged to "take charge and be fully responsible for their actions and the action of their teams."
- **Thinking**—Leaders are expected to practice "logical analysis, evidence-based problem solving, and reasoned foresight to tease out the very best ideas and find the right way forward."
- **Strategy**—Leaders are guided to demonstrate "forward thinking (the art of what's possible), creative thinking (asking new and 'better questions' to chart new ground), and objective-based thinking to find the best practical solutions to achieve our desired outcomes."

Strategy and execution are the source of the protocols which are reinforced by the ChampionGold Standard.

Those three precepts, coupled with MindChamps' ten standards of leadership—reflected in values and attributes such as optimism, resilience, emotional intelligence, decisiveness, and creativity—serve as the center of all leadership considerations (depicted in the white circle in the diagram below). These precepts and standards of leadership serve to support the important functions of leaders which are addressed in the five MindChamps protocols (the darker circles in the outer ring below).

Diagram: MindChamps 4 Precepts and Standards of Leadership (center), surrounded by: Defining Roles & Responsibilities, Recruiting & Selecting Staff, Staff Development, Building the Team, Planning for Improvement.

Specific to the roles and responsibilities of leaders, MindChamps notes:

> "PreSchool Leaders and primarily Principals have a direct responsibility for the quality of teaching and learning within each centre. This means, first of all, ensuring that all teachers are confident and skilled in delivering the

CHAPTER FIVE

unique MindChamps PreSchool Curriculum, based on the combination of the 4 powerful domains of Education, Neuroscience, Theatre and Psychology. In leading teaching and learning, leaders will also set very high expectations and provide the right conditions in which those expectations can be achieved, continuously evaluating both the effectiveness of teaching and the quality of Champs' learning outcomes. They create a learning culture which enables all of our young Champs to become enthusiastic, effective, independent learners who love to learn…in short, they become 'Champion Learners'."

From a training and learning perspective, MindChamps develops and measures its leaders on abilities associated with:
- Curriculum delivery,
- Developing learning,
- Quality learning environment,
- Modelling best practice,
- Monitoring and evaluation,
- Being 'present,'
- Learning support, and
- Behavior management.

Similarly, standards are provided for a multitude of dimensions in each of the following categories: leading culture, developing relationships and teams, planning for improvement, and managing the school. Rather than listing all of the dimensions outlined in each of these areas, I will just provide a few examples from each area to give you a sense of the breadth of standards to which leaders are trained and by which they are held accountable.

Dimensions associated with Leading Culture include but are not limited to:
- Broadcasting the vision,
- Celebrating success, and
- Cultural diversity.

Standards associated with Developing Relationships and Teams include:
- Providing support,
- Team planning, and
- Growing leaders.

Focal areas for Planning for Improvement include:
- Target setting,
- Tackling underperformance, and
- Corporate accountability.

Standards involving Managing the School include:
- Financial and human resource management,
- Response to feedback, and
- Learning resource management.

In addition to specifying the multitude of standards and offering rigorous training (so leaders can meet and improve in relation to MindChamps standards), center leadership also receives a variety of practical tools to help them facilitate the growth and development of their team members. For example, MindChamps offers guidelines on how to effectively conduct regularly scheduled teacher observations.

Leaders are instructed on how to align expectations with each teacher prior to conducting a classroom observation. They are also taught how to effectively observe a classroom with

Always believed Leadership po...
1. Quality of leading others
2. Quality of extra commitment
3 Quality of relationships

All living someone else's dream

Vision   x Gold Standard

                  Action

Set → Monday → Strategy

SMART –

granular guidance for each step in the process. For example, one MindChamps leadership tool breaks down the classroom observation process into stages. In the first five to ten minutes of observation, it instructs leaders to consider:

- How well does the teacher engage Champs from the outset?
- What are the purposes/learning goals of the lesson?
- Do the Champs understand the learning goals?
- Does everyone know what s/he should be doing?
- Is the environment/atmosphere good for learning?
- Is the level age-appropriate?
- Does the environment stimulate learning?
- Do available resources support/stimulate learning?

Leaders are encouraged to augment their direct observations with input garnered from speaking with students and through a review of students' work. These leaders are guided on how to provide constructive feedback on each teachers' strengths and opportunities for development. They are also instructed on how to incorporate classroom observation into MindChamps' well-designed Performance Management and Appraisal System.

MindChamps describes their performance management process as a:

> "...shared commitment to high performance. It helps to focus our attention, both individually and collectively, on more effective leadership, management, teaching and supervision in order to raise the centre's overall quality of teaching and learning and to benefit our Champs, teachers/trainers and the principals/centre managers.

Within the MindChamps context, appraisal is seen as a supportive and developmental process designed to ensure that both educators and Principals/Centre Managers have the expertise to carry out their roles and job responsibilities effectively. This means identifying and providing appropriate and effective personal training and development, to ensure job satisfaction and a high level of expertise and progression of staff in their chosen profession."

In addition to classroom observations, leaders at corporately-owned and franchised MindChamps PreSchools review each teacher performance by evaluating:
- Weekly lesson plans,
- Their student's portfolios and progress reports,
- Classroom educational displays and the quality of their learning environment,
- Communications with parents, including weekly updates and letters,
- Recognition and praise from parents,
- Involvement in special events, and
- Contribution to other MindChamps team members.

Leaders are then taught to meet with teachers on a regular basis to discuss each teacher's contribution against key performance indicators and individualized objectives which are co-created with them. Leaders are trained on the SMART goal-setting process. SMART is an acronym for setting goals which are: Specific, Measurable, Achievable, Reasonable, and Time-bound. Leaders also undergo a similar process of performance appraisal and action-planning in partnership with MindChamps.

CHAPTER FIVE

A Day in the Life of a Business Leader

'Giving a Warm Welcome':
Meeting and greeting staff, parents, Champs as they arrive (9 to 9.30 a.m.) – walk around the center to ensure it is safe, clean and attractive.

Management by Walking Around: Walking around the centre.
√ Smiling, greeting, exchanging warm words with all staff, Champs and visitors met.
√ Reviewing quality and condition of display in client relations and public areas.

Popping In:
Into every classroom in the course of the week for a few minutes.
√ Looking at Champs' work, the environment (E.g. reception, classroom and toilets) and the delivery of the lesson (for review with Principal if necessary).

9.00am – 9.30am:	Greeting and walking around
9.30am – 10.00am:	Connection with the principal
10.00am – 11.30am:	Attend to ongoing matters or connection with support staff (if required)
11.30am – 12.30pm:	Personal time/sales planning and follow up
1.30am – 3.00pm:	Connection Time Meetings (to attend when necessary)

Depending on the needs and the seasonal priorities (i.e. the annual appraisal exercise, projects such as the year-end concert, the business leader and the principal must connect weekly on the following key activities:

Reading and Reviewing Logbook

Strategic Planning and Review
√ 1-1 meeting with principal to review progress of the action plan and any ongoing projects.

Connection Time:
√ Join in the meeting (when necessary and periodically to connect with the team) or review of the minutes of meetings.
√ Teambuilding
√ Sharing Golden Moments (news)
√ Admin (Keep to minimum!!)
√ Discussion and peer learning of the curriculum
√ Leadership team meeting
√ Level meeting

Staff Meeting
Extended meeting to be held on Friday evening or Saturday morning for the purpose of:

- ✓ Building and bonding team
- ✓ Sharing best practice
- ✓ Planning events
- ✓ Curriculum development
- ✓ Staff training etc
- ✓ Important for the business leader to inspire the team with exciting news and developments for the center

Staff Retreat
Whole team event for the purpose of:
- ✓ Building and bonding the team
- ✓ Appreciation for the team
- ✓ Connection with team members
- ✓ Leisure based for enjoyment – *suggest to change to* Rest, relaxation & reflection (Business leader may extend to the family members of the team)

Dialogue With Parents
Special 'tea' sessions or field trips with the parents for the purpose of:
- ✓ Relationship building

109

As an education organization, one important distinction has been emphasized in relation to the development of leadership criteria and strategies. Although many leadership elements overlap between them, the skills and strategies of the Principals and education leaders are distinct from those of the business leaders, and this is reflected in the specific leadership trainings and the resources which the organization supplies for these important team-members.

Before I leave the topic of leadership development tools, I should note that MindChamps helps administrators manage their substantial workflow demands. As an example, MindChamps offers examples of efficient time management such as the one presented on pg 109 — referred to as, "A day in the life of a Business Leader."

Joseph Juran, author of the book **Managerial Breakthrough: The Classic Book on Improving Management Performance**, once observed, "Without a standard there is no logical basis for making a decision or taking action." When it comes to MindChamps, the 3-Mind Model establishes standards for curriculum design. The MindChamps ChampionGold Standard Leadership sets the bar for consistent daily operations. In combination, these tools assure transformation and growth in every interaction, every day, in every MindChamps location. That is **The MindChamps Way**!

CHAPTER FIVE

Follow the Red Dot

- When companies take a structured yet progressive approach to product and process excellence, they tend to experience heightened productivity, enhanced innovation, and sustainable business growth.
- Teachers at MindChamps are inculcating the MindChamps Education and Life Philosophy of 100% Respect and Zero Fear. What does 100% Respect and Zero Fear mean to you? How can you apply it to the way you approach other people and the challenges you face?
- MindChamps PreSchools focus on four elements associated with educational quality (curriculum, environment, teachers, and leaders).
- MindChamps designs each center to be an intentional learning environment which blends physical elements with human factors created by administrators, teachers, and other center team members.
- The MindChamps ChampionGold Standard sets clearly defined performance criteria, establishes policies and protocols, provides training for leaders and frontline team members, offers continuous improvement tools, and guides rigorous performance monitoring. How effectively have you done the same in the context of your business?
- MindChamps effectively uses a management and appraisal system which tracks the key performance indicators and individualized goals teachers and center leaders create.
- Standards drive transformation and growth at MindChamps through curriculum design and operational management. What standards do you use to drive growth and transformation in your business or life?

PART THREE
TAKING THE MOVEMENT TO THE WORLD

CHAPTER SIX
Producing Results

"One of the great mistakes is to judge policies and programs by their intentions rather than their results."

Milton Friedman
Recipient of the Nobel Memorial Prize in Economics

We've entered the final section of **The MindChamps Way**, titled **"Taking the Movement to the World."** Over the course of this chapter and the final one, we will examine MindChamps' global impact, MindChamps' likely future, and lessons you can carry forward from your time spent reading this book.

As I alluded to in chapter one while describing the "what of MindChamps," much of MindChamps' success can be appreciated by simply doing a side-by-side comparison of the company at three distinct moments in time.

1998 – MindChamps was little more than an idea beginning to take shape as a research organization.

2008 – MindChamps launched its first PreSchool and initiated the MindChamps PreSchool franchise (signing agreements to open 22 centers).

2018 – MindChamps is a well-capitalized, publicly traded company operating 74 centers in partnership with franchisees.

It sold 165 licenses and had centers in Singapore, Australia, the Philippines, Abu Dhabi, Dubai, Myanmar, Vietnam and Malaysia.

Growth numbers are an undeniable indicator of MindChamps' successful pursuit of the company's vision:

to nurture the power of human potential for a better tomorrow.

This is also clear in the company's mission to:

...challenge and improve education standards globally.

To verify that MindChamps is honoring its mission, leaders look for proof that the organization is challenging and improving the lives of students and helping develop Champion Minds, Learning Minds, and Creative Minds. They also assess progress toward their vision by determining the degree to which they are helping children realize their potential to address current and future societal needs. This chapter will give you a palpable sense of MindChamps' impact as told by parents and students. As you'll soon see, the stories told by these families resoundingly demonstrate the human side of MindChamps' movement to revolutionize education for this generation and generations to come.

The Heart of MindChamps

Throughout this chapter, I will be relying on feedback from individuals who have given permission to share their stories publicly. I recount this feedback (as it was written) under the umbrella of approval granted by MindChamps, noting that the information

CHAPTER SIX

shared here typifies extensive and equally glowing accounts, and that, in keeping with MindChamps' core value of Integrity, the organization offers no incentives to anyone who shares their story.

I've categorized these results as offering support for:
- Growth of a Champion Mind, Learning Mind, or Creative Mind,
- MindChamps' Mission, Vision, Values or Core Themes,
- Operational Excellence/Learning Environment, and
- Family Loyalty and Referrals.

Before I start, I should note that I will be primarily sharing MindChamps PreSchool results but at times will add input concerning other MindChamps programs (e.g., enrichment programs like PSLE Success or MindChamps Reading) to highlight the consistency of reported outcomes across MindChamps offerings.

Growth of a Champion Mind, Learning Mind, or Creative Mind

Let's begin by exploring what parents have to say about MindChamps' role in developing the qualities of a Champion Mind—including emotional intelligence, communication skills, self-awareness, and self-confidence. Ms. Roy Adith shares how her search for a preschool resulted in a MindChamps experience where her son substantially improved his ability to express himself, noting, "Since I didn't have any friends with preschool children, I researched online to find the best preschool for my son Neel. MindChamps PreSchool has very good reviews from many parents. For the past 4 months he has been in MindChamps, he interacts with me more when he comes home. He speaks in full sentences with proper language structure instead of mincing up his words.

He has also improved a lot in terms of conveying exactly how he is feeling, whether he is happy or sad."

One can sense how Ms. Rei Wang's daughter is gaining both communication ability and self-confidence thanks to MindChamps, as she says, "It's very exciting when you see your kids talk about the things that they feel happy about, especially since En Xi has always been a very reserved kid. So for her to express herself, it really means a lot. …As a parent having come this far with her, it's very inspiring to see this change."

Parents repeatedly share how MindChamps' staff guide them to effectively facilitate their children's growth. Julian Sin and Christabella Leon observe, "We made the right choice in putting Jaylynn in MindChamps PreSchool. The curriculum is so well-planned, enriching and holistic in developing a child. With a conducive learning environment and a team of passionate teachers, Jaylynn has grown leaps and bounds in terms of her social, thinking and problem-solving skills. She is happy and always looks forward to going to school every day!"

At a preschool level, Sohini and Benjamin-Brandon King describe similar benefits regarding their daughter's confidence and expressiveness, sharing, "Our daughter loves attending MindChamps PreSchool. We have seen her grow into an independent toddler, as she makes new friends and learns to express herself confidently."

Since we've highlighted how parents experience interpersonal and fundamental character shifts on behalf of their children (in keeping with the Champion Mind), let's look at how MindChamps fuels a child's desire to learn and fosters academic success.

CHAPTER SIX

Learning Mind

Peter T. holistically describes the expansion of his son's learning ability, noting, "During my son's three fruitful years at MindChamps PreSchool, I witnessed tremendous growth in both his cognitive and social development. He enjoyed his lessons very much and was immensely fond of his teachers, who were uplifting… the dedicated teachers at MindChamps had taken great care of my son's overall well-being. I am extremely pleased with them. Also, my son is coping well in Primary 1…due to the crafted learning programmes—meticulously prepared by MindChamps for him."

Ms. Diong Lang Shi (whose son participated in MindChamps' Thinking Cap Programme —geared to enrich students in Primary 3 to Primary 6), credits her son's success to MindChamps' ability to teach him how to learn, noting, "I'm very impressed with the philosophy behind MindChamps. I'm a lecturer myself and understand the need for students to have the right mindset to persevere and succeed in school and in life. Not only is this programme about study skills, more importantly, it's about coaching and mentoring. My son is now more self-disciplined as a result of it. MindChamps' Thinking Cap Programme is the coaching programme that all students need!"

When it comes to actual academic performance, MindChamps enrichment programs repeatedly translate to greater academic mastery. For example, Ms. Chole Lau reports that MindChamps helped her son achieve score improvements (D to A in Science and B to A in Chinese), noting, "Things changed for the better after we enrolled Enson in the MindChamps programme. With a well-designed curriculum in place and a team of passionate and committed trainers to guide the students, Enson is now more positive towards learning... Over time, he was able to absorb new concepts and information more effectively as he could better understand what was taught."

At this point in the chapter, we've exclusively heard from parents. But what do the students who have attended these types of MindChamps programs have to say? Elaine Goh, a PSLE Success alumna shares, "I was really happy I got 4 As for my PSLE! It's a large improvement from what I got before I started the MindChamps programme, which were B for Chinese, a C for Science, and D for Math. ...MindChamps has helped me develop my Champion Mindset and now I believe I'm a Champion too!" In similar fashion, MindChamps alumna Pearlyn Wee notes, "When you take up a programme at MindChamps, you will see a change in the way you think, the way you do things and the way you see others. I learnt many powerful study techniques and now I find my studies to be so much more interesting! I am so glad that my grades improved after attending MindChamps—I scored 4A* on my PSLE." Quite the testimonial: "a change in the way you think, do things, and see others." What more could we ask of education?

You've read about how parents and students view MindChamps' impact on character, as well as social and academic growth. Let's take a moment to examine the role MindChamps plays when it comes to enhancing creativity.

Creative Mind

In chapter two, we explored how leaders have historically underappreciated the importance of creativity, viewing it to be illusive and intangible. Conversely, in chapter four, we discussed how MindChamps' leaders conceptualize the Creative Mind as

CHAPTER SIX

imagination directed toward creative purpose and how they seek creativity in the context of innovative solutions. As such, parents of MindChamps' students frequently report their children demonstrate outcome-focused creativity. For example, Ms. Lynn Lee notes, "Through the MindChamps Writing Programme, Jovan has gained more confidence in his speech and is now more imaginative in his writing. His teacher has definitely made an impact on his improvement. She also has been encouraging Jovan to read more books during his free time." Similarly, Mr. and Mrs. Cheng note, "MindChamps PreSchool is an excellent preschool…Its educational pedagogy does not restrict any inspiration and imagination from children – rather, they have moulded, amplified and enhanced these skills. Our experiences thus far have surpassed all of the expectations that any preschool can offer. I see a variety of traits that my son has picked up, such as self-confidence, creativity, having a Champion Mindset and strong social skills."

Theologian and poet John Henry Newman observed, "Growth is the only evidence of life." When it comes to the evidence offered by MindChamps parents and students, it's clear experiences at MindChamps have enlivened the growth of the Champion Mind, Learning Mind, and Creative Mind. Let's look at how MindChamps team members are facilitating this growth by living MindChamps' mission, vision, values, and core themes.

Demonstrations of MindChamps' Mission, Vision, Values or Core Themes

For years, I have been writing about branded customer experiences. For me, a brand is essentially what customers (in MindChamps' case, it's the students and parents), say about a company. To be successful, a company's intentions (reflected through mission, vision, values, and core themes) should be discernable in the perceptions of those they serve. At MindChamps, parents often describe interactions that reflect MindChamps primary value: heart.

In her description of MindChamps, Rachel H. specifically uses the word love, as she shares, "I am very thankful to Charlotte's class teachers for their exceptional work with Charlotte. What they have done has far surpassed my expectations. Under their love and guidance, Charlotte has blossomed into a buoyant little girl with a vivacious appetite for knowledge and is always keen to tell me what she has learnt in school."

Much like Rachel's use of the word love, Mrs. Yvonne Seah also speaks of MindChamps' heart by using words like care and warmth, noting, "My daughter Rianne has been with MindChamps since she was 21-months-old. Initially she was reserved and cried every time I had to leave her at the centre. However, after just one week, she became happy and excited to attend school with her friends and teachers. The staff's (including the logistics staff) care and warmth made the difference. Under their nurture and monitoring, Rianne has grown not only in the aspect of academic knowledge and skills but also social and psychomotor skills, related to movement or muscular activity associated with mental processes. As a parent, I am assured of my child being in good hands. As an educator, I have confidence in the staff and their competencies."

MindChamps' secondary value—integrity—also emerges from parent descriptions. In the case of Jayanthie and Ram, this integrity is reflected in the way MindChamps team members fulfill their promises, sharing, "We were looking for a preschool that has a strong team of experienced teachers who could assure us that

CHAPTER SIX

they are confident in helping our son overcome his apprehensions. We discovered MindChamps Preschool. During our visit, we shared our concerns with the centre staff and teachers, who then assured us that Dillon would be in good hands. True to their words, they have journeyed through numerous highs and lows with us and have proven their abilities beyond expectation. Today, Dillon has blossomed into a confident, articulate and sociable boy who enjoys going to preschool. We truly owe these achievements to the teachers who continue to play a role in Dillon's development. In particular, we would like to express our sincere gratitude to his teacher who goes above and beyond her call of duty and works tirelessly with us to ensure that Dillon has a fun yet effective learning experience as a preschooler."

As MindChamps team members act in accord with the company's core themes and live its values of heart and integrity, parents notice! These types of actions, in turn, support MindChamps' mission to "*...challenge and improve education standards globally*" in pursuit of the company's vision "**to nurture the power of human potential for a better tomorrow.**"

Operational excellence, curriculum, and learning environment

Throughout chapter five, I highlighted MindChamps' strengths with regard to curriculum development, ability to foster a learning environment, and the company's overall operational excellence. These elements are certainly registering with parents. Feng Wenfu and Irene Tham reflect on the physical and human elements of MindChamps' overall learning environment, noting, "When we first stepped into MindChamps, we knew this was the right environment to nurture our child during the early years. The clean, spacious and bright classrooms with its thoughtful layout offer the little ones ample and comfortable space for optimal learning and socialization. Play is crucial in early childhood and their huge school playground provides a safe outdoors environment within the school that stimulates children to use their creative energy in healthy interactions with one another. We remember our son having a difficult time transitioning from home to school initially. Under the nurturing and respectful care demonstrated by all the teachers and staff, he has blossomed into a confident and articulate young boy, who also knows how to extend love and kindness to those around him. We are indeed proud and grateful to have witnessed remarkable progress in his academic, physical and socio-emotional development. Thank you, MindChamps!"

Adelynn Queck focuses her comments primarily on MindChamps' thoughtful, effective curriculum and how teachers infuse passion into its delivery, sharing, "I love MindChamps' teaching pedagogy. This school practices high standard methods as they allow the kids to have fun while learning. The teachers are very devoted to their jobs, they did a fantastic job in looking after Lucas with great patience… I have seen my son grow so much, as he can perform tasks like making his bed, showering and putting on his clothes, independently. Signing Lucas up to MindChamps was definitely a right decision. I would highly recommend this school to anyone that cares about their children's future."

Expression of Loyalty

Walt Disney once said, "Do what you do so well that they will want to see it again and bring their friends." There are two separate

CHAPTER SIX

elements in Mr. Disney's wisdom. The first involves the importance of earning a customer's repeat business and the second relates to securing a customer's referral. Parents of students at MindChamps demonstrate both loyalty and a willingness to refer others to MindChamps.

From the perspective of loyalty, Mr. Wilson Tan and Ms. Catherine Seet report, "After seeing how our daughter had benefited from MindChamps, we decided to send our son too — he has been transformed; he's now more positive, doesn't give up when faced with problems, enthusiastic about studying and willing to sit at his desk for longer periods of time. We strongly recommend the MindChamps Thinking Cap Programme to all families."

Once a parent has a successful experience with a child enrolled in MindChamps, it is reasonable that they would enroll their other children. However, trusting your own children to a preschool is very different than referring others to attend. Do people really refer family and friends to MindChamps programs? Ms. Chloe Lam resoundingly says, "Yes!" Ms. Lam notes, "I didn't choose MindChamps PreSchool, my children did. They told me they really like the school. I have seen an enormous improvement in them, for the teachers are dynamic, dedicated and they handle my children with utmost care. I have already recommended two of my friends to MindChamps PreSchool!"

Some parents don't need a recommendation; they make their decision to send their children to MindChamps based on the impact they observe in the lives of others. Bai Jian Liang reports, "We enrolled Zelene in MindChamps Reading after seeing great improvement in her cousins who were taking other programs in MindChamps. Zelene was very happy after her first lesson and was very much looking forward to her next lesson. We are really satisfied with her improvement; she has opened up and talks more about her classmates and teachers, her English literacy skills have also improved greatly, and she is now more independent than before."

Novelist and short-story author Philip Roth noted, "Seeing is believing and believing is knowing and knowing beats unknowing and the unknown." Throughout this chapter, we have shared what parents and students have seen and come to know about MindChamps. They have provided a glimpse into the results MindChamps is producing. These results support the insights I've sought to provide in prior chapters (e.g., company culture, mission, pedagogy, and learning environment in operational excellence). Through the words of these parents and students, it is quite clear that MindChamps has taken their revolutionary educational movement to the world, and that the movement is progressing meritoriously—**The MindChamps Way**.

CHAPTER SIX

Follow the Red Dot

- In keeping with the advice of Milton Friedman, we should not judge policies and programs by their intentions but rather by their results.
- MindChamps' results can be demonstrated in the company's rapid success and expansion.
- Brands are defined by the shared perceptions of those they serve. By that definition, what are people saying about your personal and business brand?
- Parents offer rich examples of how MindChamps fosters the Champion Mind (reflected in students developing emotional intelligence, communication skills, self-awareness, and self-confidence).
- Students and parents express gratitude for MindChamps programmes which help students develop learning skills, become more eager to learn, and improve overall academic performance.
- Parents report that MindChamps helps learners channel imagination into purposeful creative work.
- MindChamps' mission, vision, values, and core themes can be easily identified in the comments of parents. This suggests that MindChamps team members are actively demonstrating behavior in keeping with MindChamps' cultural objectives. How are your mission, vision, and values surfacing in what your customers are saying about you?
- Operational excellence in MindChamps' curriculum development, learning environments, and management system are delivering perceptible benefits to parents and children.
- Excellence drives loyalty. Loyalty enhances referrals. Loyalty and referrals fuel sustainability and the growth of a brand, a movement, and a revolution.

CHAPTER SEVEN

Shaping the Future

"I believe our legacy will be defined by the accomplishments and fearless nature by which our sons and daughters take on the global challenges we face."

Naveen Jain
Founder and Former CEO of InfoSpace

A fellow U.S. based consultant and author called me recently and asked, "What book are you working on?" I responded, "I am taking the MindChamps movement to the world." He then said, "You're taking the what to where?" and then added, "I know Starbucks, Mercedes-Benz, and all the other companies you've worked with and written about, but what is the 'MindChamps movement'?"

I am not sure my colleague was prepared for my answer. I told him about David Chiem and how David's childhood experiences created a desire to do great things in the world. I talked about David's lifelong pursuit of learning and how he expressed himself creatively. I explained that David sought out world-renowned experts and researchers in the fields of education, neuroscience, psychology, and theater as part of a research organization that he established in Australia in 1998. I traced the evolution of MindChamps over the next decade and spotlighted the launch of the first MindChamps PreSchool and the MindChamps franchised PreSchools in 2008. I gave him an overview of the people behind the MindChamps brand, the strength of its mission, vision, values, and social charter. I shared the 3-Mind Model that serves as the foundation for the MindChamps curriculum and told him about their Champion Gold Standard. In closing, I offered him proof of the brand's success based on its global growth, capitalization, and healthy franchise model. I also shared what parents and students are saying about MindChamps.

Some 20 minutes later, my colleague stopped me and said, "I should have just asked to read the book." My friend was correct: I attempted to use that phone call to pack in as much information as I've sought to share with you in the pages of this book.

In addition to kindly listening, my colleague did me an unexpected favor when he asked his question. He helped me realize that while I have known David Chiem for almost a decade, others (like my colleague in the United States), are yet to fully appreciate the MindChamps' history and the likely long-term significance of the brand.

I sent this book to my colleague and I sincerely hope it will deepen his understanding (and the understanding of every reader) concerning David's vision for MindChamps. I also hope readers garner respect for what David and his colleagues have accomplished over the past two decades both for MindChamps and more broadly for education. More importantly, I hope **The MindChamps Way** serves to illuminate the need for global change in education—so that our children are better prepared to succeed in the 21st Century.

CHAPTER SEVEN

Staying Ahead of the Curve

One of David Chiem's signature statements runs: "At MindChamps, we must always stay ahead of the curve, but never ahead of ourselves." It is an aphorism that underpins the organization's consistent focus on realistic improvement and growth.

Any conversation with David Chiem or Brian Caswell about MindChamps' approach to the pursuit of their long-term goals, or their philosophy, inevitably leads to the notion of evolution.

As Brian Caswell puts it, "If education is a response to, and a toolbox for, interaction with a constantly-changing society, then any successful educational model must be predicated, at its heart, on a philosophy of what we call 'purposeful evolution'.

"This means that, as 'a place of the future', we have always planned in terms of MindChamps 1.0; MindChamps 2.0; MindChamps 3.0 and beyond, as a way of deliberately focusing on moving the 'big picture' forward."

And perhaps that is the real key to MindChamps' success.

My Crystal Ball for MindChamps' Future

While we are approaching the end of the final chapter in this book, MindChamps as a company is in the early chapters of its success story. MindChamps is gearing up for huge growth. The company's leaders are carefully and tirelessly evaluating all prospective franchisees that present partnership opportunities. Given what has happened in the last decade, it is hard to imagine what MindChamps will look like ten years from now. I wouldn't be surprised if there are many other business books written about the success of MindChamps over that period.

As I look to the company's foreseeable future, I envision MindChamps will continue its hypergrowth and widen its global impact. Despite MindChamps leaders telling me that they are not focused on a specific geographic footprint, I anticipate that the reputational strength of the brand will create openings for it in places well-beyond its current geographic reach. It's difficult to imagine a place where the brand's value proposition wouldn't be needed.

Given the commitment MindChamps leaders have to exemplify Champion, Learning, and Creative mindsets, I see the company continuing to leverage the insights of global thought leaders and cutting-edge technology as it incessantly improves teaching tools and product opportunities. The MindChamps culture and emphasis on teacher training should continue to help leaders attract and develop human talent across the globe. From a risk perspective, I will be watching for MindChamps' ability to scale in the face of burgeoning demand. Obviously, this risk is mitigated through its ChampionGold Standard management system, its Teachers and Leadership Academies, its franchise model, and the fact that the drive to maximize the potential of the human mind is built into the very DNA of the organization.

The past six chapters have demonstrated what success can look like in the area of education, but talk to David Chiem, and you quickly realize that what has been achieved so far is only, by his standards, the beginning of the story — 'MindChamps Version 1.0'. True to his philosophy of Trinity Leadership, the Thinking and Strategy that have fueled the growth of the organization so far, have already spawned the strategy which will carry the '3-Mind Revolution' on into the future.

CHAPTER SEVEN

MindChamps Version 1.0 encompassed the original research phase; the development of the 3-Mind philosophy, strategies and techniques; pilot programs and, ultimately, the implementation of the breakthrough S.M.I.L.E.S. preschool curriculum.

Focus on the preschool stage first was, as David describes it, "…a function of tackling the most difficult, and most important challenge first."

Why 'the most difficult?' Simply because it was the area with the least empirical evidence or historical focus to support real curriculum development.

Brian Caswell sums it up succinctly, when he explains, "The S.M.I.L.E.S. model is a breakthrough, because its focus is on creating a teacher mindset — an understanding that early-childhood cognitive development is holistic and integrative, so the experiences that build the cognitive networks should be holistic and integrative, too."

It is the S.M.I.L.E.S. curriculum that forms the foundations for the evolution of integrative 3 Minds curricula for older children in the 'MindChamps World Schools', which are already in development for Primary, Secondary and Tertiary students.

As Brian Caswell describes it, "Learning strategies, mindsets and social skills develop slowly, as children build their 'evolving narrative' of the world, creating enough cognitive connections to, eventually, process abstract concepts and develop sophisticated reasoning. In the preschool context, we are engaged predominantly in 'laying the foundations' for the future development of the 3 Minds."

Originally standing for 'Sensory, Motor, Intellectual, Linguistic, Emotional and Social', The S.M.I.L.E.S. approach views every activity, from structured play to diaper-changes, as an opportunity to simultaneously stimulate and integrate all six of these essential 'S.M.I.L.E.S.' fields.

It is, as Caswell describes it, "the culmination of Mindchamps version 1.0."

But, in 'big-picture' terms, it is also an ideal metaphor for the evolutionary processes at work within the wider organization.

If MindChamps version 1.0 was about foundational research and program-development; systems and strategies, In line with the mission statement: '**to challenge and improve education standards globally**', 'MindChamps 2.0' is about '**the empirical evaluation of efficacy, the on-going implementation of new research-based strategies and the publishing of those strategies for improvement in educational processes worldwide**'.

The establishment, in 2018, of the 'MindChamps A.I.R. (Applied Integrative Research)' Unit — represents an exciting new empirical research initiative, which will lay the foundations for the next generation of MindChamps curricula. Embracing the latest advances in neuroscience, psychology, technology and educational research, A.I.R. provides the opportunity to map, and learn from, the developmental and educational outcomes of new MindChamps initiatives.

It has already led to the creation and beta-testing of an evaluation tool to establish and measure the world's first C.C.Q. (Creativity and Champion Mindset Quotient) to gauge the development of a child's potential in these two key areas of the 3 Minds.

It also draws on the work of Brian Caswell, David Chiem and Professor Allan Snyder FRS, in the area of 'Narrative Intellect'.

CHAPTER SEVEN

The subject of an up-coming paper, Narrative Intellect is described as:

"…the uniquely human ability to make meaning through the association, accumulation and sequential ordering of elements. It transcends mere story-telling, and even verbal language – to present as a fundamental principle of intelligence in all its forms, including, for example, the mathematical, the musical and the spatial. Narrative is the mental representation within which all sensory inputs are processed and synthesized and through which all thought is understood and expressed. As such, it qualifies for the designation of 'the unifying principle of human intelligence'."

Such research has led to a small, but crucial, refinement in the definition of the S.M.I.L.E.S. model itself. From a model which focused on the development of teacher mindset to create 'integrative strategies', it becomes a model which employs integrative strategies to lay the cognitive foundations for the development of the 'integrated mind'.

MindChamps A.I.R. and the 'MindChamps 2.0' strategy of evaluating efficacy and advancing standards is an essential part of the evolutionary mindset driving the organization. It is also the foundation upon which version 3.0 will be built.

Already in the planning and development phase, the third incarnation of this education revolution aims, in the words of the MindChamps founder, to "…create a new frontier for learning, changing the nature of the classroom and the role of the teacher in response to the opportunities afforded by Virtual and Augmented

Reality, Artificial Intelligence, Machine Learning and CGI [Computer Generated Images].

"In a world where Artificial Intelligence is fast becoming the norm, the classroom as we know it today is already an historical artefact and the challenge of engaging the young minds of tomorrow requires a quantum leap. That is what our Versions 1.0 and 2.0 have been preparing for. From the beginning, we have always predicted that tomorrow's pedagogy would not be about imparting content — or even critical thinking — for an AI teacher can perform that task efficiently and cheaply.

"In the classroom of tomorrow, the teachers of tomorrow will be mentors and coaches, nurturing human values and developing the Champion Mind, the Learning Mind and the Creative Mind with compassion and empathy."

By combining insights drawn from two decades of work within the domains of neuroscience, psychology and education with their expertise in film, theatre, literature and the creative arts, MindChamps has created the ideal opportunity to leverage on advances in technology to create the classroom of the future today.

It is a classroom where children will be empowered to explore and discover; to question and be questioned; to work at their own pace or collaborate — across the room or across the world — a place of growth and engagement, with teachers who, freed from the strait-jacket of purveying content, have evolved into expert facilitators of learning; observers and expediters of individual development.

Following the MindChamps model 3.0, imagine tomorrow's children exploring the wonders of science together with Einstein, Newton or Galileo; mathematics with Pythagoras; Art with Da

CHAPTER SEVEN

Vinci or music with Mozart or Madonna, or where they will learn to love language and literature, one on one with Shakespeare or J.K. Rowling.

Science fiction? An idealistic techno-fantasy? Not according to David Chiem.

"Much of the technology already exists," he points out, "and new technologies are emerging constantly. In Ready, Player One, Steven Spielberg imagined the negative potential of rampant technology in a dystopian world. At MindChamps, we are envisioning the positive use of the same powerful force to open up a universe of life-enhancing learning. The potential for education in such an environment is almost unlimited.

"Comparing this opportunity with traditional education is equivalent to the difference between having a primitive, stand-alone computer on your desk, or the latest solid-state gaming machine, with terabytes of storage and a powerful search-engine, connected to the net with high-speed optic fiber."

But, as the team at MindChamps understands only too well, technology alone is not the answer. Rather, it is the platform upon which the new model of 21st Century learning, from the womb to the grave, can be built.

'MindChamps version 3.0', when it emerges, will be the offspring of 20+ years of research and development and a creative mindset that sees the gaps and has the entrepreneurial vision and craft to fill them.

Like all great brands, MindChamps will need to maintain its focus on its mission while facing all the unavoidable challenges that come with explosive growth and expansion. Whenever I try to predict the future of a company like MindChamps, I am reminded of 6th century wisdom shared by poet Lao Tzu, who cautioned, "Those who have knowledge, don't predict. Those who predict, don't have knowledge." As such, I will end my predictions and turn to a subject that is much more knowable, which is how you can continue your revolutionary journey with MindChamps.

Your Return on Investment with MindChamps

You have invested your money, and likely an even more precious commodity, your time, in this book. As such, I have a responsibility to assist you in maximizing your return on those investments. If you are a parent who lives in a community in which MindChamps operates, I recommend your follow-up include a visit to a MindChamps center to learn how MindChamps might serve your family. If you are an entrepreneur, the best sequel to this book might be for you to scroll to the bottom of the mindchamps.org home page. From there, you can click on the "franchise enquiries" link. Upon completing the enquiry form, you can explore how to bring the MindChamps movement to your community.

If you are a parent who does not have a MindChamps nearby, you may want to share this book with local educators to foster a discussion about **The MindChamps Way** or, better yet, read David Chiem and Brian Caswell's book, **The 3-Mind Revolution—A New World View for Global Leaders, Educators, and Parents**. Pass **The 3-Mind Revolution** around your community and pick up one of the parenting books written by David and Brian. These titles include, **The Art of Communicating with Your Child—Strategies for Inspiring the Champion Mindset in Every Young Person** and **Pre-school Parenting Secrets: Talking With the Sky** (in collaboration with Kylie Bell).

CHAPTER SEVEN

For those of you who read The MindChamps Way exclusively as a business profile book, I recommend you share it with other leaders in your company. Consider using the "Follow the Red Dot" sections to prompt discussions and to begin a process of action planning. While the opportunities for discussions extend beyond what I can list here, you might consider some of the following suggestions:

- Compare and contrast your business strengths to that of MindChamps,
- Assess the Champion, Learning, and Creative mindsets of your leadership team,
- Revisit your mission, vision, and values to assess their brevity, clarity, level of aspiration, and how easily they are remembered,
- Create a social charter,
- Readily share your mission, vision, values, and social charter with your team members and customers,
- Explore ways to drive emotional intelligence, communication skills, self-awareness, and self-confidence throughout your organization,
- Re-examine your operational and service standards,
- Evaluate the efficiency of your management system and the overall consistency of your deliverables,
- Review what your customers are saying about your brand to assure you are on-mission, and
- Consider your onboarding and training processes to drive an understanding of your mission and vision, as well as the rehearsal required to serve customers on your brand stage.

Whether you read **The MindChamps Way** as a parent, educator, entrepreneur, business manager, or frontline service provider, I hope you will view your investment in this book with a learning mindset. It should serve as a foundation to foster further growth for your family, your business, your community, and/or education globally. For me, concepts presented in books can best be addressed with guidance imparted by martial arts expert and cultural icon Bruce Lee when he said, "Absorb what is useful, Discard what is not, Add what is uniquely your own."

The MindChamps Legacy

I have asked great leaders at the brands about whom I've written to share the legacy they hope to leave. Horst Schulze, the founder of the modern-day Ritz-Carlton Hotel Company said, "I want to deliver perfect service. Not excellent service but perfect service. It is through striving for perfection that excellence is achieved." As CEO for Mercedes-Benz USA, Steve Cannon, shared, "We will be driven to delight every customer. That will be my legacy." The longtime CEO of Starbucks, Howard Schultz, noted, "I want to build a lasting brand that elevates lives—one cup at a time."

I will pose that same question to you (please accept it in the spirit of MindChamps' 100% Respect, Zero Fear philosophy, which, you will remember, is MindChamps' way of nurturing "students to have full confidence in themselves, while considering the rights and opinions of others". What legacy do you hope to leave? I understand the question is audacious and whom am I to ask? Moreover, what makes any of us think we will leave a legacy? In truth, all of us have impact. Some will create that impact by design and others will have it happen by default. There will be those who will garner a modicum of success. Others, like Horst Schulze, Steve Cannon, Howard Schultz, and David Chiem will achieve significance.

CHAPTER SEVEN

The magnitude of our significance will likely be a function of our effort, our scope, and our mindset. In part, our significance will hinge on our courage to express our vision for the future. I hope you will take a moment to thoughtfully answer the legacy question and share that answer with someone you can trust—to help you realize your potential to make it possible. For me, the question of legacy can often be approached by considering an observation from philosopher and psychologist William James. James noted, "The great use of life is to spend it for something that will outlast it." What do you want to spend your life doing such that your efforts will outlast you?

When I asked David Chiem to answer the legacy question, he humbly said, "I am not seeking a legacy. I want to start a conversation—a conversation about realizing the dream that prompted me to start MindChamps. It is the dream reflected in our mission, vision, and social charter. My hope will be that MindChamps starts a conversation about what might be possible if people work together to challenge and improve educational standards globally and, in the process, what might they achieve if they seek to create educational opportunities where those opportunities would not otherwise exist. I believe MindChamps contributes to that conversation and I will continue to steward us in that direction. My hope is that others will engage that conversation in partnership, and we can all explore possibilities in our society and in our homes. I further hope that this conversation will continue on past my leadership and past this generation. I have always believed that the story of MindChamps, in a hundred years time, will continue to be told."

A special thanks to David and the other leaders at MindChamps for letting me play a small part in advancing their conversation. I also owe a debt to you for reading this book to its end. Your dedication, persistence, and commitment to lifelong learning reflects a Champion's Mind. I trust you will creatively take what you've learned to move David's conversation forward—**The MindChamps Way**!

About the Author

Dr. Joseph Michelli helps business leaders and front-line workers create differentiatied branding, compelling brand stories, high-performance cultures and "craveable" customer experiences. His consulting services, presentations, and publications show leaders how to engage employees, elevate human experiences, master service skills, and innovate relevant customer solutions.

To achieve these measurable outcomes, Dr. Michelli provides:

Keynote speeches

Workshop presentations

Panel facilitation

Leadership retreats

Customer experience diagnostics

Consulting services targeted at culture change and customer experience elevation

Dr. Michelli, the chief experience officer of The Michelli Experience, has been recognized globally for his thought leadership on customer experience design, as well as his engaging speaking skills, and influential impact on service brands. In addition to The MindChamps Way, Dr. Michelli is a New York Times, Wall Street Journal, USA Today, and BusinessWeek bestselling author who has written:

The Airbnb Way: 5 Leadership Lessons for Igniting Growth through Loyalty, Community, and Belonging

Driven to Delight: Delivering World Class Customer Experience the Mercedes-Benz Way

Leading the Starbucks Way: 5 Principles for Connecting With Your Customers, Your Products, and Your People

The Zappos Experience: 5 Principles to Inspire, Engage, and WOW

Prescription for Excellence: Leadership Lessons for Creating a World-Class Customer Experience from UCLA Health System

The New Gold Standard: 5 Leadership Principles for Creating a Legendary Customer Experience Courtesy of The Ritz-Carlton Hotel Company,

The Starbucks Experience: 5 Principles for Turning Ordinary into Extraordinary

Humor, Play and Laughter: Stress-Proofing Life With Your Kids

CHAPTER SEVEN

Dr. Michelli has also coauthored When Fish Fly: Lessons for Creating a Vital and Energized Workplace with John Yokoyama, the former owner of the World Famous Pike Place Fish Market in Seattle, Washington.

For more information on how Dr. Michelli can present at your event, provide training resources, or help you elevate your culture and/or customer experience, visit www.josephmichelli.com.

Dr. Michelli is eager to assist you drive delight for your people and customers. He can be reached through his website josephmichelli.com, by e-mail at patti@josephmichelli.com, or by calling 001-727-289-1571.